The Power of One

Pursuing Unity and Purpose in the Body of Christ

Anthony Pelt

To my "Baby Doll," Millicent, for encouraging and supporting me on this journey;

To Imani, Ty, and Hope—you are great children;

To Mom and Dad for keeping me near the cross;

And to Radiant Living Worship Center and Florida-Cocoa Church of God—We are Radiant and Cocoa strong!

CONTENTS

Note from the Author

Welcome to *The Power of One: Pursuing Unity and Purpose in the Body of Christ*! Following each main chapter of this book, you will find a workbook section that includes reflective questions and application-oriented "action steps." These questions and practical steps are intended to help you as you make Christ, and unity in His church, your number-one priority.

The workbook sections are meant for potential use in independent reflection, group study, discipleship training, or simply discussion with a friend. If you keep a pen handy as you go through these sections, you can write down your thoughts and record notes in the areas provided.

No matter what prompted you to pick up this book, I hope it will encourage you to seek your identity and purpose in Christ and His Body—in the power of One.

—*Anthony Pelt*

INTRODUCTION

Can I Get a Witness?

One of the main reasons why many of us today find it difficult to witness to others is that we have not tapped into the power of One. Many of us have never witnessed to a living soul, and one reason we've never witnessed to anyone is because we aren't sure what to witness about and how exactly to do it.

Someone will ask us, "Can you tell me about Jesus?" We shuffle our feet and look at the ground and say, "Yeah, He's all right."

Someone will ask, "What do you know about Jesus?" Our response again, "Oh, Jesus? He's all right."

Vague responses like that may be okay for the first time, but at some point, we need to get to the heart of the matter and to tell people about the whole point and purpose of Jesus.

Here's the reality: Jesus is the center of it all. But before we can express that to people, we have to grasp it ourselves and submit to the power of One.

When a Jehovah's Witness knocks at my door, the conversation that I have with him is about Jesus. I take the opportunity to let them know who He is and help them understand what He has done. This prayer that Jesus utters in John 17 allows us to do that—it allows us to come into alignment with God, to advance in the things of God, and to share His message with others in a meaningful way.

It keeps us, also, from getting duped or running amok in our message. We are in line with God, through Jesus, and we can be confident that the words we speak and the message we bring are His, not ours and not the product of the enemy's—that is, Satan's—meddling.

This power of One allows us to show others through word and deed that God sent Jesus as the savior of this world—that He is the Way, the Truth and the Light, and that no one gets to the Father except by Jesus. That is the message; that is the abundance added to our lives through the power of One.

I realize that many people feel that they can't bring this message to their workplace—you can't talk religion on the job, or you could get fired. I realize that many today believe it's not politically correct to bring up the name of Jesus in social situations—after all, there are so many other religions out there that it's simply not politically correct to say Jesus is the only way. People will call you a fanatic, a hatemonger, short-sighted, intolerant.

The fact is, though, that Jesus saw this coming. He saw it with the disciples who physically walked with Him then, and He saw it in the future, with us, the disciples who walk with Him today. This is what makes the prayer in John 17 so important and relevant even today.

It is this prayer that allows us to connect with the power of One, to unite with God through Jesus. It allows us to share the Good News of His salvation despite the circumstances, the peer pressure, the disapproval, the hostility, and the politically correct climate that we face today.

We are saved. We are going to heaven because of what Jesus has done, and Jesus gives us the ability to make that proclamation through His prayer for protection and productivity in John 17. It is through Him that we can access this awesome power of One, if we are willing to do so.

The reality is that we do have a choice. We can give ourselves over to the power of One, or we can refuse to do so. God won't force us. Sadly, too often, people get attendance at church confused with salvation through Jesus. People sometimes get so caught up in the personality of the church they attend—the prestige of the church, the comforts of the church, the popularity of the pastor, and so forth—that they start to look to the church for salvation. The church actually becomes a substitute for Jesus.

The truth is, though, no matter how good a church is, that church cannot save you. Only Jesus can.

The church can, unfortunately, be a distraction, lulling us into a false sense of security: "I attend church every Sunday, I sing in the choir, I give a tithe, I serve when I'm needed—it's all good, then." But it's distractions like this that often keep people from experiencing the power of One.

They believe that going to church is "good enough" when in reality, it is the cross they need to go to—it is to Jesus that they need to surrender themselves to align with God. The church is not going to do that for them. Only Jesus can save.

Of course, there's nothing wrong with going to church—it is a place where we can express the joy of salvation with others, and worship as a community. But the danger happens when the church becomes our substitute and our excuse for not seeking the power of One that Jesus intended for us to have when He prayed that prayer in John 17.

Let's be clear, the world needs to have an impression and an impact put on it from Christ. People need to see that Jesus can transform people in a way that no church ever could. That power comes from His unity with the Father. Jesus was, and still is, able to take those on whom others have given up and transform them into the persons God intended them to be. How many times do we see Jesus do this throughout His recorded ministry in the Bible?

Consider the story of how Jesus found a man possessed by demons among the gravestones in a graveyard. The story in Mark 5:1–20 tells us that Jesus meets up with a man who wanders among the burial caves, so strongly possessed by demons that chains and shackles can't even hold him down. The people have given up on him and believe that he is beyond help.

It doesn't matter to Jesus what the people think. He goes to that man, and he confronts the demons holding the poor man captive. There are so many of them that they call themselves "legion." So Jesus is literally facing an army of demons—but Jesus has the power of One.

He is One with the Father, and He orders the demons to leave the man. Jesus sends them into a herd of pigs, and the pigs run into the water, drowning themselves.

Jesus restores the man on whom everyone else had given up. But then what happens? Does the man just go about his normal life, returning to whatever job he did before he was possessed?

No! The one on whom everyone had given up goes off to the ten towns of that region, proclaiming the Good News of Jesus Christ. He taps into the power of One, recognizing that Jesus' unity with the Father—the same oneness that allowed Jesus to face down an army of demons—was available to him as well.

CHAPTER ONE

Unity

Neither I pray for these alone but for them also which shall believe on me through their word, that they may all be one, as thou, Father, art in me and I in thee, that they also may be one in us; that the world may believe that thou hast sent me. And the glory which thou gavest me, I have given them; that they may be one, even as we are one: I in them, and thou in me, that they may be made perfect in one; and that the world may know that thou hast sent me, and hast loved them, and thou has loved me. Father, I will that they also, whom thou hast given me, be with me where I am; that they may behold my glory, which thou hast given me: for thou lovedst me before the foundation of the world. O righteous Father, the world hath not known thee, but I have known thee, and these have known that thou have sent me. And I have declared unto them thy name, and will declare it: that the love wherewith thou hast loved me may be in them, and I in them. — John 17:20–26 (KJV)

Focus. It's a small word, but it says a lot. Take, for example, Kentucky Fried Chicken. Their motto some time ago was "We do chicken right." And there's truth to that.

Why? Because chicken is their focus. They don't offer hamburgers or hot dogs or fancy sandwiches. They offer chicken. Sure, you can go to some other chains that offer all that other stuff and get a chicken sandwich. But it's probably not going to be as good because chicken is not their primary focus. They're too busy dividing their energy among all the other menu items to give much attention to their chicken sandwich.

But at KFC, they have perfected the way they do chicken because it's all they do.

What's the point of this? Is this book in fact a thinly veiled advertisement for a fast food chain? No. The point is that we, as Christians, need to have that "KFC" kind of focus.

We need to be clear that we do one thing—follow Christ. We should be careful not to get distracted by all the other stuff that's on everyone else's menu because our one main focus is Jesus Christ. Ultimately, we need to be absolutely clear, to ourselves and to others, that we are undivided, undeterred, and undistracted in our mission as Christians.

What is that mission? To be radiant, radical, and righteous—to shine and to soar to the glory of God.

The Lord's Prayer for Us

Having that singular kind of focus is not easy. In fact, it may be downright impossible unless we first do one important thing: ask God for help.

As humans, we are limited in our ability to focus on Christ alone. We are easily distracted by the dozens of other things demanding attention in our lives: family, jobs, money, houses, cars—all those things we chase after that command our attention. But with the help of God and the Holy Spirit, our vision becomes clearer and our focus is turned in the right direction.

The more we focus on Christ, the closer we come to becoming all that He's commanded us to be, all that He's *apprehended* us to be, all that He truly wants us to be in this earthly realm.

When we approach that place where our focus on Christ is so sharp we can begin to see what He sees in ourselves, we then begin to understand the true concept of unity. Only then can we can take the next step and ask God to help us understand the true nature and power of One—the strength of unity that Jesus Himself expressed in John 17.

Of all the prayers that Jesus uttered in the Bible, we tend to refer to the disciples' prayer—the "Our Father"—as the Lord's Prayer. In reality, though, I believe John 17:20–26 should more aptly be called the Lord's Prayer. It is a prayer that Jesus Himself prayed to the Father, and is probably the longest prayer of Jesus recorded in Scripture.

The prayer itself is filled with passion because, as Jesus is praying, He knows that He is about to go away. The Last Supper is over and He is about to be betrayed by one of His own followers, handed over to be arrested, tortured, tried, and crucified.

Communion has happened. Jesus is now about to be taken and tried. He's about to be crucified. Basically, Jesus is saying, "Father, I realize that if I don't get this prayer to you that your name may be extinguished—that the enemy may interfere and prevent these disciples from telling others the Good News. The enemy may stop them from spreading the Word and the truth."

Most of us have played a game I know as "telephone line." Someone at the start of the line whispers a bit of information into the ear of the next person in line. That person passes the information along to the next person, and so on and so on, until the last person then states out loud the information he has received.

Usually, though, by the time the last person repeats what has been passed down to him, the information bears no resemblance to what was originally said, much of it having been lost or distorted in translation.

This is the game the enemy wants to play with the message that Jesus brings. The enemy figures that if he cuts off the main source of this information—Jesus— then the message will never get passed down correctly and the Good News will be lost in translation.

Jesus sees this coming, so He intervenes with the Father. He asks Him to ensure that His message never dies. That is the basis for the prayer found in John 17. This prayer is also known as the Great High Priestly Prayer, and it shows a side of Jesus that many times we take for granted:

Jesus is our intercessor.

Back in the days that Jesus walked the earth, the job of the priest was to take the sacrifices of the people and offer them up to God. The average person was not worthy to offer the sacrifice and had to turn it over the Priest as one who could approach God on their behalf and offer the sacrifice for them.

In the same manner, the only way and the only reason that we can go to God the Father in prayer is because Jesus, the Son, is our intercessor. He is the One who serves as High Priest and goes before the Father, ensuring that our prayers are acceptable. Jesus takes our words, our actions, and our desires and makes them acceptable to the Father.

In John 17:20–26, Jesus prays for this to be possible. He prays for the power of One, asking that we can access it, accept it, and be united with Him so our prayers can be heard by the Father, just as Jesus' prayers are heard. This is the Oneness—the unity—that is so essential to us as Christians.

Focus on Unity

Keep in mind that unity is not the same as uniformity. God never commanded us to be uniform. He doesn't want us to dress the same, act the same, speak the same, do the same things, or look the same way. But God does expect us to be unified.

He's asks us to be in unity. He expects us to be together—to be unified as one body—regardless of our differences. He also understands that, given our nature and our tendency toward self-centered behavior, the only way that this unity could be accomplished was through His supernatural power.

The Bible asks, "Can two walk together, except they be agreed? (Amos 3:3 KJV). This is a problem for us as human beings. We tend to disagree a lot. Even if we each think of one person with whom we get along famously— with whom we agree on almost everything—the fact is, there will still be disagreements. We will never agree with another person on absolutely everything.

So, how can we follow the command of unity? There is only one way, and that is through the power of the Holy Spirit. We need the Holy Spirit to help us to walk together and be agreed.

Here's the reality: many people wonder why the church, as a whole, can't get together and be unified as one. Why are there so many churches, so many different denominations? No one ever wonders why there are so many different gas stations, or donut shops, or coffee shops. But people tend to worry over the fact that there are so many different churches, and they use that fact to say that the church, as a whole, is disjointed.

Is there truth to this?

God tells us that the reason for this so-called schism is that many believers have not yet tapped into the power of One.

The church—God's church—has one purpose on this earth, and that is to reveal the unity of God. The problem, though, is that many believers have yet to realize this and are still caught up in the competition of church versus church. They are working toward the singular goals of their own autonomous church but are not working toward God's ultimate goal of unity.

When you consider it, unity is absolutely essential for any kind of real achievement. It's our outline—our blueprint. It's needed for a successful family unit: for a family to be happy, there needs to be unity among its members. A family that is not unified quickly becomes fractured and dysfunctional, and the happiness of togetherness is lost.

For a business to be successful, there needs to be unity. Employees need to be working together toward a common goal and need to get along in doing so. If there is backbiting and ill will among the employees, generally, the business suffers and business goals are not met.

Unity is needed for government to function. We've seen firsthand what happens when those in government don't get along and can't agree—nothing gets done. Laws don't get passed, budgets don't get approved, and everything seems to grind to a halt.

The same is true for sports teams. When the players on a sports team get together, they have to play as one cohesive unit, or they will lose. The minute those players start chasing their own agendas, the team falls apart. It's only when they play together—each fulfilling their individual roles on the team with an eye toward one unified common goal of the team as a whole—that they can win the game.

My favorite football team is the Pittsburgh Steelers. I don't have any real connection with Pittsburgh, yet all my life, I've loved the Steelers. All throughout football season, on game day, I'll wear my Steelers jersey. I'll talk about how great the Steelers are, how they are the best football team in the world.

But just because I wear the jersey doesn't mean I'm on the team. Sure, I talk about them a lot, support them, and cheer for them, but I'm not on the field with them.

I'm not in the huddle. I'm not running plays with them. My enthusiasm has no effect whatsoever on the outcome of the game. I'm literally sitting on the bench, the sofa, or the comfy armchair, watching, while I pursue my own personal agenda.

The sad reality is, in the same way, there are a lot of people wearing "Christian jerseys," but they have no real skin in the game. They are not on the field running the plays. They sit back and watch, cheering on the team, while they pursue their own personal agenda.

They are missing out on that "oneness," that unity with the team that has a genuine effect on the game. The world does not see Jesus in them because they are not out on the field—not a real part of the team.

Protection and Production

The truth is that Jesus prayed the John 17 prayer, first and foremost, for our protection. He knew that the moment He left, the enemy would come in like a ravenous wolf, ready to devour His followers. Even Simon Peter, who was chosen to be the Rock by Jesus, was not immune.

Peter loved Jesus, no doubt, but given his background and temperament, if you caught Peter on a bad day, he'd curse you out, no questions asked. Jesus recognizes this and basically says, "Father, if he acts like this while I'm right here with him, how bad will it be after I'm gone?"

Judas, in the meantime, was working on a deal to betray his friends for money, while James and John, the "Sons of Thunder," were trying to call down fire on their enemies. Jesus sees all this and recognizes that if God does not give them some kind of supernatural protection, they will ruin themselves.

So Jesus prays for their protection. But then He says He doesn't just want them to be protected—He wants His followers to be *productive*.

Why? Why not just pray that they receive protection and stay safe? Wouldn't that be enough?

Of course not! The reality is that Jesus' followers were a living epistle. People were reading them, watching them, and learning about Jesus through their actions and behavior.

What we need to realize is that what was true then is still true now. We, as followers of Jesus, continue to be a living epistle. People are still reading Jesus through us. Every day, whether we realize it or not, we are sending an instant text message to the world with our actions and our behavior. What does that text message say? Does it give the world mixed messages? "I love God and I love Jesus, but I hate you—stay back at least 50 feet"—that would not exactly be a message unity, would it?

But it's our human nature, isn't it? To give mixed messages—to root for the team but stay on the sidelines?

So Jesus said in His prayer (and I am paraphrasing), "I have to pray for protection for My followers, but Father, I must pray that they stay productive, because the world is corrosive, the world is crooked, and in a world this crazy, even good people do dumb and cruel things."

After all, that is why Jesus died in the manner He did—because people in that crowd decided to crucify Him. And even the ones in the crowd who didn't really want to crucify Him fell prey to the suggestion and pressure of the others around them who were yelling, "Crucify him!"

Some people in that crowd who might have never considered the option of crucifixion suddenly had their eyes opened to that possibility, and were swayed by the crowd. Those whom Jesus had healed, who were lame and walked, who were mute yet spoke, might have been swayed to join the crowd's cry: "Crucify him!"

God recognized that the world is fickle and that people are subject to its influences. Jesus recognized that if His followers were not protected first and foremost, they would never be productive.

Becoming One

Let's be honest. Most of us are not that accommodating toward others. We are, by nature, self-centered creatures. If I cook a meal for someone and that person comes in, looks at it, and says, "Really? Is that what we're eating?" my first reaction is not to go back into the kitchen and cook them something they would like more.

My reaction would likely be a little harsher than that—if they don't like what I made, then they can go eat a box of crackers instead. It's that "take it or leave it" attitude that often works against the Oneness that God needs us to experience.

Jesus knows that our nature, apart from Him, would never be changed. Apart from Him, we could never be transformed. In His prayer, he essentially says, "Father, they must now understand the reason I functioned as well as I did was because I Myself was subject to the power of One. I am One with You."

Jesus wants us to experience firsthand the power of One. I love this about Jesus. Anything Jesus prayed for came to pass.

In John 17:11, He says, "And now I am no more in the world, but these are in the world, and I come to thee. Holy Father, keep through thine own name those whom thou hast given me, that they may be one, as we are" (KJV).

Basically, Jesus is acknowledging that He is about to physically leave this world and is concerned for the disciples He leaves behind, who are still in the world. He is asking that they might experience a sense of oneness that He Himself experiences with the Father.

He wants us, as His disciples, to experience that incredible intimacy He shares with the Father and to be able to experience that with one another as well.

In using His relationship with the Father as an example of the type of oneness He desires, we can see that He is talking about more than just being good friends, walking side by side with each other. Rather, He is asking us to be supernaturally One.

There is no relationship on earth to which Jesus can compare this, so He uses His relationship with the Father—a relationship in which He completely yields Himself to the will of the Father—as the example that He wants us as His disciples to follow.

In yielding Himself so completely to the Father, Jesus becomes an empty vessel to be filled entirely by the Father. This is true Oneness, which is what He wants for us—not just the disciples who were physically present with Him then, but those who would follow Him in the future as well, including you and me. This prayer was meant for us. In John 17:20–21, Jesus says:

> *Neither pray I for these alone, but for them also which shall believe on me through their word; That they all may be one; as thou, Father, art in me, and I in thee, that they also may be one in us: that the world may believe that thou hast sent me.* *(KJV)*

Again, in using Himself and His relationship with the Father as an example, Jesus is saying that He doesn't just want us to be "one" as we might understand it. He also wants us to go beyond that and have the same supernatural Oneness He shares with the Father.

However, this point is critical: we can't access the power of that kind of Oneness except through Jesus. We cannot be One with the Father without Jesus. He is the point of connection, the Intercessor, the One through whom we are made acceptable to the Father.

The power of One gives us access to unimaginable potential to be the Christians who Jesus intended us to be. I know some really nice people who are good Christians, but they are "blah" Christians. The reason they are stuck in that rut of being "blah" Christians is that they have yet to access the power of One. They have yet to make that connection.

In John 17:23, Jesus goes on to say, "I in them, and thou in me, that they may be made perfect in one; and that the world may know that thou hast sent me, and hast loved them, as thou hast loved me" (KJV). Jesus is talking about a certain kind of maturity. He is asking that, at a certain point, we as His followers will be able to comprehend what He is saying.

It's kind of like math. We may see a math problem and be able to solve it, but do we really understand the principles behind it? Jesus wants us to understand the principles behind this Oneness. He wants us to understand there's a principle that applies to us, the Father, and the Son—a powerful, supernatural equation that only comes into play when we access the power of One.

We're not talking about some abstract, metaphysical concept. In our society, the enemy has taken that phrase "metaphysical" and turned it into something spooky and abstract to the point where nothing is acceptable. People will refuse to believe something because they just can't figure out what it means. That's the enemy creating confusion.

Consider that when we draw the number one, it's actually an earthly representation of what Jesus is telling us. First of all, '1' is a symbol of alignment. It is a singular, straight line. So, the power of One brings us into alignment.

The number one is also the first whole number of advancement. If we add zero to something, it stays the same. But when we add the next number, the number one, whatever we add it to increases. These may seem like simple concepts, but many of us never quite grasp them as they apply to what Jesus is saying.

The power of One means, first, that we are in alignment with God. Once we are in alignment with God, then we are automatically increased—we are added to. Without this alignment, we can never have the increase, and we never seem to advance in things of God.

The Bible asks us how it is that we still need to be taught the rudimentary concepts of our faith—that we need to be taught the very basic ABCs—when we should be at a place where we are the teachers (Hebrews 5:12).

The answer is simple: because we have not yet yielded to the power of One. We have not yet completely emptied ourselves and given ourselves over, heart, mind, body, and soul to God, to be aligned with Him and advancing in Him.

The number one also represents abundance. All it takes is one to have more. So, when we align ourselves with God through Jesus, this leads not only to advancement in the things of God, but also to our own abundance. We are added to; we are made richer in God.

Jesus recognizes that if His disciples can access the power of One, they will be saved from faltering and falling. They will come into alignment with God. Even Peter, the hothead, will line up. So will doubting Thomas—he'll line up. The same will be true for tumultuous James and John—they, too, will line up. Jesus knows that if these men can get tied into the power of One, they will turn the world upside down. They will go out into the world and be witnesses to the Good News, and their message will change everything.

But they can only do this if they are tied into the power of One—if they are unified with God through Jesus.

This access to the power of One was the crucial difference for these disciples of Jesus. Just look at what they accomplished—how they were able to witness despite the circumstances in which they found themselves.

Keeping this in mind, though, let me remind you that Jesus was not only praying for them: He was also praying for us. What He expected of His disciples then, He still expects of us today.

DIY Doesn't Work

Consider for a moment another story in the Bible, found in Matthew 17:14–21, after Jesus goes up onto the mountain and experiences the transfiguration. He has left His disciples by themselves for a bit. During that time, a man asks the disciples of Jesus to heal his son, who is possessed by a demon.

When Jesus returns, the man is upset because the disciples haven't been able to heal the boy. Jesus, however, drives out the demon and the boy is healed.

What happened? Why couldn't the disciples help the boy? Jesus later tells them that it was because they had so little faith (Matthew 17:21). Faith in what?

Faith in the power of One.

They were trying to do it themselves, not aligning themselves with God through Jesus. They were fooling around with something that they should have taken to Jesus. The power of One allows us to bring everything to God.

We may not have people come to us with their demon-possessed children. But if we are not careful, there will come a time when a person who needs to hear the Good News of salvation will come to us and we will have nothing to offer. Why? Because we are not unified with God through Jesus—because we have not tapped into the power of One.

Too many of us are stuck on the belief that we have to do it ourselves. That's what our society teaches us: we have to be strong, independent, and self-sufficient.

Jesus tells us something different. We need to be dependent on Him, on the power of One, in order to be strong. That's why He prays what He does in John 17—because He knows our tendency to rely on our own abilities, as well as the necessity for us to rely on God instead. He knows we need help aligning ourselves with God and accessing the power of One.

Keep in mind, though, that Jesus doesn't pray this prayer so that we, as His disciples, might be glorified. Far from it. Instead, He wants us to glorify the Father through what we accomplish by the power of One. The purpose of the power of One is to release the glory, and the glory belongs to God.

In John 17:22, Jesus says He releases the glory: "And the glory which thou gaveth me, I give to them" (KJV). We need to look at each other as Christians, as followers of Christ, and ask, "Where's your glory?" It should shine out from us, so clearly that everyone can see it. Then we can be seen as unified in alignment with God's will—the power of One.

The Bible says it like this: "That if two of you shall agree on earth as touching any thing that they shall ask, it shall be done for them of my Father which is in heaven" (Mathew 18:19 KJV). That's the power of One; that's the power of agreement and unity.

But, here's the key: Jesus also tells us, "for without me ye can do nothing" (John 15:5 KJV). The power is of One, and that One is God. Without alignment with God, we can do nothing. Apart from Him, we can do nothing. Yet with Him—in unity with Him—all things are possible.

The people in many churches today don't seem to get this. Too many church leaders go about as if everything depends on their will and their desires. They go about their business as if they have the power to do anything apart from God. They do things designed for their own glory, not for God's glory—not in unity with God's purposes. And such things are destined for failure.

The truth of the matter is that God wants us all to line up—to get in sync with Him. And when we do, it releases tremendous power in our lives.

Stop pretending that we have the power to do anything apart from Him, and surrender instead to the power of One. Our souls should glow with God's glory so that everyone can see it. When we enter a room, people should know we're there, not because of our own presence but because of the presence of the Holy Spirit. When we leave a room, people should notice that we've gone—again, not because of our charming nature, but because of the light we bring in glory to the Holy Spirit.

We need to understand, though, that light also brings bugs. Have you ever been outside and when you turn on the lights? The moths come by almost immediately. When we attach ourselves to the power of One, our souls will glow with God's glory—and the moths will come, including demons, devils, and temptations of every kind.

But we're not in it alone. God is there with us because we are aligned with Him through Christ. There's no need for us to be afraid. Jesus tells us that "these signs shall follow them that believe; in my name shall they cast out devils; they shall speak with new tongues" (Mark 16:17 KJV).

That's power—the power of One.

WORKBOOK

Chapter 1 Questions

Question: What is one way in which greater unity is needed in your local church? How can you help to promote unity in this respect?

_____
_____
_____
_____
_____
_____
_____
_____
_____
_____
_____

Question: How is uniformity different from unity? Where do you see uniformity threatening unity in the church?

_____

_____

_____

_____

_____

_____

_____

_____

_____

_____

_____

_____

Question: In what areas of life have you been trying to "do it yourself"? How, specifically, will you begin to surrender this area to God?

_____

_____

_____

_____

_____

_____

_____

_____

_____

_____

Action: Let the Lord's prayer for us—that we would have unity—be your prayer as well. As a member of the Body of Christ, focus on unity in Jesus even more completely and passionately than KFC focuses on chicken! Remember to seek unity without demanding uniformity. Rather, become an empty vessel for His love, as He intended, and let Him be your protector while you focus on being productive in Him. In short, align yourself with Christ and lean on Him instead of trying to do it yourself—because doing it yourself never truly works.

Chapter 1 Notes

CHAPTER TWO

One Thing

One thing have I desired of the LORD, that will I seek after;
that I may dwell in the house of the LORD all the days of
my life, to behold the beauty of the LORD, and to enquire
in his temple. — **Psalm 27:4 (KJV)**

Psalm 27 is a beautiful Psalm written by King David, and is a declaration of faith in the Lord—a declaration of Oneness. In Psalm 27:8, David writes, "When thou saidst, Seek ye my face; my heart said unto thee, Thy face, LORD, will I seek" (KJV).

That is a declaration of focus. With everything else going on around him, all the other distractions—and in David's time, there were plenty—David declares that he will stay focused on the face of God and seek God first in all things.

It goes back to our previous KFC analogy. When you walk into KFC, there are no other choices—no other distractions. There's chicken. It's what they focus on. It's their specialty. In this Psalm, David is making God his specialty—his primary focus and first in all that he does.

The Number-One Priority

All God's people have an enemy—Satan. The enemy knows that if he can keep us divided, diverted, and distracted, we'll never move into our destiny.

That's not to say people aren't moving forward in life; many people are moving, but they're going in the wrong direction. They're relying on their own judgment, their own power, and are trying their best.

But in reality, they become more and more disjointed, to the point they become frustrated. They can't function, and they can't be fruitful. Why not?

Because they're trying to do this thing called life on their own, with no real connection to the God who is the author of their destiny. They are not in alignment, and they have lost their true focus.

The Word of God tells us, "But seek ye first the kingdom of God, and his righteousness; and all these things shall be added unto you." (Matthew 6:33 KJV). That's a pretty clear statement and a very clear promise.

Yet the enemy has us seeking anything and everything *except* the kingdom of God. He lures us away, convincing us to go after other things—money, jobs, clothes, relationships, video games—all those things that keep us busy and distracted and keep our focus off of God.

Many of us who have children know that every now and then, we must remind them to mind their own business. Kids will try to find out things and get involved in things that don't concern them, in which case we have to tell them, "Keep your nose on your face, not over there."

Sometimes, it is the same with us. We stick our noses into places where they don't belong and, in so doing, take our eyes off of God. We need to mind our business, and our business should be all about God.

We need to be about one thing. We need to quit looking around and quit trying to be in everything. There are times when God will tell us, "Listen, I've got a planned path for you. I have a destiny for you, and you don't have to be everywhere, trying to do everything." So the concept of "one thing" is a critical concept to the hearts of believers.

The "one thing" should be that which keeps us rooted and fortified, secure in the knowledge that we don't have to be tossed to and fro by every wind, wave, or doctrine that comes along. We have a firm grasp on the reason we are here, and we have a steadfast focus on doing that which God calls us to do. One thing.

Consider for a moment what Jesus says to the rich young ruler in Mark 10:21. The man asks Jesus what he needs to do to inherit eternal life. He already follows all of the rules and commandments but wants to know what else he could do. Jesus answers him by saying:

> *...One thing thou lackest: go thy way, sell whatsoever thou hast, and give to the poor, and thou shalt have treasure in heaven: and come, take up the cross, and follow me.*
> — *Mark 10:21 (KJV)*

The problem was, the young man was so rich that he had many things distracting him, competing for his attention, yet he was missing the one thing he needed: focus on God. Jesus wanted the young man to sell everything—to get rid of all the distractions—and focus only on Him.

But the young man could not do it, so he had everything except the most important thing.

The same thing can happen to us. We can be so distracted by everything else that we miss the next opportunity for God to bless us. We miss out on the good things God has in store.

Back when I was getting ready to confirm my Master's, I realized I was missing one credit-hour. How that happened, I don't know. I suppose I just wasn't paying close enough attention. But they told me I was missing one credit-hour, and without it, I couldn't get the degree. It didn't matter how much work I had done; it didn't matter how many A's and B's I had gotten. I was not allowed to walk on stage to accept my degree because I was missing one thing.

One thing can make all the difference. Why in the world would we do all that we do, go through all the hardships we go through, and then not be able to partake in that which we say we want? That's what will happen when we are distracted, not paying attention, and fail to focus on that one thing.

We get so tied up in the things of this world that we forget what it's really all about. But material things will fade—cars break down, clothes get moth-eaten, and money loses its value. All of those material things for which we strive so hard eventually break down and become worthless.

So, why do we focus on them instead of focusing on what's eternal? Jesus pointed that out to Martha in Luke 10:38–42. The Bible tells us that Jesus went to visit Martha and her sister Mary. Martha was busy cooking and cleaning during Jesus' visit, whereas Mary just sat at the feet of Jesus, focusing on Him and listening to His teaching. Martha got a little mad about this, because she was doing all the work while Mary just sat there.

But Jesus said to her, "Martha, Martha, thou art careful and troubled about many things: But one thing is needful: and Mary hath chosen that good part, which shall not be taken away from her" (Luke 10:41–42 KJV).

Jesus basically tells her, "Listen, don't you dare be mad at Mary because she is focused on the One thing that it important, while you are focused on all the other stuff that doesn't matter." Mary was focused on the eternal, while Martha was focused on all the other stuff. Martha wanted Jesus to come to her house, I'm sure, but when He did, what happened? She didn't pay any attention to Him because she was so busy with all the other distractions of life.

Many of us are the same way. We beg for God to be present in our lives, and then, when we finally get His attention, we are not there with Him—our focus is on everything else, and not on God's presence.

Don't get me wrong. Going to church is a good thing. Still, if we go to church because of the worship team, or because we like the pastor, or because we are friendly with the people, we are going to church for the wrong reason. We need to attend church for One reason: because of God's presence. Then, in turn, we need to be present there for Him.

And we don't have to be in a church, either, to be in God's presence. In the year King Uzziah died, Isaiah still saw the Lord. John was on a prison island called Patmos, yet he said, "I was in the Spirit of the Lord's day..." (Revelation 1:10 KJV).

How can God's Spirit be found in all of these different places? Because God's Spirit is in *us*. No matter where we are, no matter what our circumstances, we can still be all about that One thing—blessing God.

Finding Our Destiny

For many of us, because we are so divided and so diverted, we never even get a taste of our destiny. We never see our destiny. That's a sad thought.

At the beginning of every new year, people typically make resolutions, which usually have to do with getting improving somehow. The truth is, though, we are not going to become better, no matter how many resolutions we make, unless we focus on the One thing.

As believers, we need to say, "If I'm going to help Your kingdom, Lord, help me to be all about One thing."

Paul said it like this in his letter to the Philippians:

> *Brethren, I count not myself to have apprehended: but this one thing I do, forgetting those things which are behind, and reaching forth unto those things which are before, I press toward the mark for the prize of the high calling of God in Christ Jesus.*— **Philippians 3:13 (KJV)**

Paul says that he has one purpose and that yesterday is gone. Yesterday was great, and everybody probably has a story to tell about it. I used to play the saxophone, and I think I played all right. But I have to admit, when I tell my stories about yesterday, my playing seems to get better and better as the years go by.

The point is, you can't live in yesterday. If we rest on the laurels of yesterday, we'll never be fruitful today. If anything, yesterday is only a springboard to help us get to tomorrow.

As believers we need to ask God to keep us from foolishness. Foolishness distracts us and keeps us falling into the trap of foolish pursuits, but God helps us to stay focused on the One thing.

Oftentimes, a period of prayer and fasting can help us stay away from foolish pursuits and keep us focused on God. Nobody really enjoys times of fasting, but since the beginning, prayerful fasting has been a tool used by believers to eliminate distractions and sharpen their focus. When we find our lives spinning out of control, and we find ourselves being more easily deceived and distracted, we should consider prayer and fasting as a way to help us get back on track—back to a place where we can hear the divine call and fulfill our destiny.

Lack of destiny or desire will lead us to forsake the One thing and will make us double-minded. When we are double-minded, we are unstable. In fact, James said it like this: "A double-minded man is unstable in all his ways" (James 1:8 KJV).

Our inability to focus on One thing means that other things will become corrupted. Our lack of focus divides us against ourselves. Luke 11:17 tells us that a kingdom that's divided against itself will always fall, and that applies to our personal selves as well. When we become divided against ourselves, we will fall.

God doesn't want us to be divided, neither against ourselves nor against each other. Division and double-mindedness cause confusion. God is *not* the author of confusion; that's the enemy's tool. Rather, when we align with God, there should be clarity in our minds—a secure stability that leads to a sense of calm, peace, and joy.

We know our Redeemer lives, and we know we've been saved for something. We know God has something great for us, and we should not become confused or confounded. Instead, we should focus on the One and on what He has called us out of our sin to do.

God did not pull us out of darkness so we would live in darkness. No. To the contrary, He translates us into His marvelous light. Yet we've got to be serious about One thing.

That means we may have to reorder our priorities. We may have to tell some people "no" so that we can tell God "yes." What does that mean, exactly?

We may have to break off a relationship that is unhealthy for us. Or we may have to tell the guys we can't play softball on Sunday morning because we have church. Or we might have to turn down the invitation to go out to the movies with the girls so that we can attend our Bible study instead. Or maybe instead of playing on Facebook or Instagram, we should set some time apart at night to do some praying.

Whatever it is that we give priority to in our lives over God, we have to let it go and put God first in thought, word, and deed.

Sometimes my name and my reputation carry some weight. Because of my position, I get invited places that maybe I wouldn't otherwise go. But there are times when my wife's name is the one with the clout. She is well known and well respected, and I carry a card around with her name on it for those situations when her name gets me where I need to be.

I have a Starbucks card, a 7-Eleven card, a grocery store card—basically, I have every one of those plastic cards we put on our key chains to get us special perks. But in certain places, it doesn't matter what cards I have on my keychain because if I don't have that card with my wife's name on it, I don't get in.

That's a bit like it is in heaven. People present all kinds of credentials to the Lord: "Don't you know me, Lord? Don't you remember me? I have this, and I've got that—and I've got this, too!"

Yet God will look at those people and tell them point blank, "But you don't have Jesus. He's the only One who can get you in. And I don't see Jesus with you at all, so you're not getting in."

If you don't get serious about the One thing, you'll never move forward in your life. No matter what you do, you'll keep finding yourself back at square one.

The game Sorry was popular when I was a kid. It could be a very frustrating game because of the way it worked. Those of us who are familiar with it know that just when we think we're getting ahead, and maybe even winning the game, we get sent back to square one and have to start all over.

Without clear focus on the One thing, our lives will be like a Sorry game: we will climb and try to get ahead, but then we will slide backward and have to start all over. It will become a vicious cycle, and we will never really get anywhere—until we get serious about the One thing.

God desires that we stay focused on Him and that we be on fire to fulfill His purpose. Romans 12:11 tells us that we need to be fervent in spirit, serving the Lord. That's what God desires—that we make Him our number-one priority and serve Him with great enthusiasm.

God has given us all good things, and He wants to give us more good things. However, we must order our priorities and put Him first in our lives. We need to serve Him with a desire that His name be lifted high so others can see all the good He has in store for His children.

In a world where people want everything they see and go running off in every direction, looking for fulfillment, we need to be the ones who shine with the light of God's presence—so that they can see His love, His power, and His goodness through us. The way we do that is simply by being about One thing.

Clear the Clutter

In Psalm 27, we are re-introduced to David. David is known by many attributes in the Bible: David, son of Jesse; David, the unifier of Israel; David, the killer of the bear and lion; David, the one who slew Goliath; David,

THE POWER OF ONE · 43

the worshipper, who spoke the words, "The LORD is my shepherd…" (Psalm 23:1 KJV); David, the worker, who built a house for the Lord; David, the warrior, ready to fight.

In this Psalm, though, we find David at a point in his life when he realizes he is stretched too thin. He comes to the realization that he has become so busy with other things that he is blinded—he can no longer see what God has called him to be.

So in Psalm 27:4, David basically asks the Lord to help him simplify his life.

You might be familiar with the acronym KISS, which means, "Keep It Simple, Stupid." It really should be, "Keep It Simple, Saints!"

The Lord tells us that if we have food to eat and a little bit of clothing, we should be content, because riches will grow wings and desert us. Building a life around *things* will result in us being left with nothing.

I've had people come to me and tell me, in all honesty, "Pastor Pelt, you know, before I came to your church, I was in business, making lots of money, but I was never happy. I was always looking over my shoulder. I never seemed to have enough."

What point is there to have a business that dominates our lives and steals our joy? Money, power, fame, material goods—too often, we become a slave to the things that we thought would make our lives easier. Why? Because we lose sight of what's really important. Like David, we become blinded to the One thing.

David realized that he had become distracted by his desires. That's why Solomon asked the Lord at one point not to give him riches. If we look at Proverbs 30:9, we find that Solomon was wise enough to realize that riches would distract him from the Lord.

By the same token, though, he asked the Lord not to make him poor, either, because then he might be tempted to steal. Rather, he asked God to give him enough to keep him focused on One thing.

Many of us, especially in today's day and age, are in sensory overload. We've got the spiritual version of attention deficit disorder. We have so much stuff going on around us!

Some people cannot play video games because the overload of stimulation causes them to have seizures. Similarly, I'd say that some of us are in a state of spiritual seizure, because there is so much happening around us. How do we get out of that rut?

One solution is to simply unplug. When we feel like we're being bombarded by all that's around us, we have to find a place of quiet where we can turn it all off and just focus on the One thing—focus on God.

I used to have asthma. When I would have an asthma attack, it was scary and overwhelming. I couldn't breathe, and as I found myself struggling to breathe, I'd panic, and that made matters worse. To help me, they would come into the room with a metronome, and the metronome would click, click, click in time. They'd say to listen to the rhythm, to focus on it; and I would close my eyes, shutting out all other distractions, and focus on the rhythmic clicking. As I did, my panic would subside, my lungs would relax, and I'd be able to breathe again.

If we want to do something great for God, we sometimes have to say, "God, help me to clear the clutter and focus on the passion of Your heart. Then I will be aligned to You and will be able to breathe and live."

From Psalm 27 we know that when we come to God, we have to be direct in our desires. In Psalm 27:4, David says, "One thing have I desired…" (KJV). He tells us that having a desire for God leads to direction. When we seek the Lord—when we have a real desire for the Lord—the Lord provides guidance.

I always tell people that if you find something you truly want to do, the Lord will show you a way to do it. It's amazing, and it's true! When people have a true passion and desire to do something, they start looking for opportunities, and they usually find them.

God tells us that when we truly desire to live holy—not just paying lip service or making a half-hearted commitment, but maintaining a real, genuine desire—He will provide the pathway to holiness. When we truly desire to do something great for His kingdom, He will provide the opportunity. But we have to make the first move. We have to move ourselves in that direction, and the way we do that is through focus on the One thing.

Let's keep it real, though. The devil doesn't really know the path our lives will take, but he knows when we start moving forward. And he doesn't want us to move forward! He will put obstacles in our way to keep us standing still, and he may even push us back a few steps.

That's why in verses eleven and twelve David says, "Teach me thy way, O LORD, and lead me in a plain path, because of mine enemies. Deliver me not over unto the will of mine enemies: for false witnesses are risen up against me, and such as breathe out cruelty" (Psalm 27:11–12 KJV). David knows that the Lord will provide direction and make a path, but he also knows that the enemy will throw obstacles in his path and try to distract him once again.

But David desires to rely on the clear direction and protection of the Lord. In fact, in Psalm 27:2, David acknowledges that in times past, when he has put his faith in the Lord, the Lord caused his enemies to stumble and fall. He knows the Lord will not let him down, and he relies on that promise.

The Lord assures us that if we let Him be our focus, or desire, our enemies won't have anything on us. That doesn't mean they won't try to distract us, dissuade us, lead us away from our desire. But when we align with God, like David says in this Psalm, we have nothing to fear—God will provide our defense.

Intimacy with God

In Psalm 27:4, David sings, "One thing have I desired of the LORD, that will I seek after; that I may dwell in the house of the LORD all the days of my life, to behold the beauty of the LORD, and to enquire in his temple." (KJV).

Let's break this down a bit. First, David is telling us what his desire is: he wants to dwell in God's house. That suggests something of a closeness, doesn't it? After all, in order to let people live in our homes and share our personal space, we have to have a desire to be close to them, don't we?

God wants us to have the desire to get close to Him and, like David, to dwell in His house. Can we even imagine the joy and beauty that awaits us in the house of God? God, who is pure goodness and love, wants to share His house with us!

Many of us, though, ignore this opportunity. We let the pressures and pursuits of life get in the way of accepting His invitation, which is ironic. After all, we spend our days chasing after all of these things we think will lead to joy and fulfillment—when the real source of joy and fulfillment is staring us in the face. But we are blinded to it because of all of these other distractions.

In this Psalm, though, David recognizes that God's presence brings purpose to his life, and he wants to dwell there, in God's presence, *all* the days of his life—not just on Sundays or holidays or when it's convenient for him, but every single day. That word 'dwell' indicates a stationary position, like a plant or a tree—unmoving and permanent. David is saying that he wants to reside in God's presence at all times, and he doesn't want to be moved. He wants it to be a permanent condition.

How can believers say, "In *everything* give thanks" (1 Thessalonians 5:18 NKJV)? How can we say, "I will bless the LORD at *all times*" (Psalm 34:1 NKJV), or "Surely goodness and mercy shall follow me *all the days of my life...*" (Psalm 23:6 KJV)? How can we say these things?

Because, like David, a true believer dwells in God's presence on a perpetual basis. They reside in God's purpose. They remain in Him every second of every minute of every day. It's not a temporary, once-in-a-while thing. It is a constant, continuous state.

In addition to dwelling in the house of the Lord, David wants "to behold the beauty of the LORD..." (Psalm 27:4 KJV).

I'm somewhat jealous of a few people in the Bible because they were able to live out this verse and actually behold God's beauty. Moses, for instance, got to run with God. Everybody was acting crazy down in the valley, but Moses got to commune with God.

Enoch did this, too. He literally went walking with God, and the Bible tells us that God enjoyed his company so much that He took him away to be with Him (Genesis 5:24; Hebrews 11:5).

Abraham was a friend of God, so much so that God created a whole new name exclusively for Abraham to use—Jehovah Jireh, which means "The LORD Will Provide" (Genesis 22:14).

In addition to beholding God's beauty, though, David also wants to "enquire in his temple." What does that mean, exactly? Simply this: David wants to learn God's principles. The word 'enquire' means to learn. David wants to learn about God, about His plans for him, about His purposes. He wants to learn how to live by God's standards.

If I may state the obvious, this world is not getting any better—if anything, it's getting crazier, and current technology plays a large part in this craziness.

During the Christmas shopping season in 2013, some people who shopped at Target found out that all of their money was gone by the end of the day because somebody used the wonders of technology to steal their credit card numbers.[1] We hear all the time about computer hackers stealing private information and about how cell phones can be rigged to detonate bombs. Airlines sometimes have to shut down operations because of computer glitches.

I had a good friend who told me recently that if I ever have to undergo surgery, I shouldn't let them do any type of robotic surgery. First, I asked what in the world that was. Then I asked, "Why not?"

I was told that another friend had undergone surgery done by a remotely operated robotic arm, and things did not go well at all. In fact, the poor person almost died. Instead of making things better, technology, in this instance, made it worse.

My point is, we may think that the human race is getting wiser with all these advances in technology, but if anything, the human race is becoming more wicked. Bizarre things are happening. All we have to do is watch the evening news to see the latest madness that is transpiring.

But David said, "I desire to enquire in Your temple." He desired to learn how to live a worthwhile life in a wicked world.

How do we do that? How can we live a life that gives glory and honor to God when trouble and strife abound?

David had the answer. He desired to dwell in the house of God, to live in His presence and learn His principles. That is how he found peace in the midst of the chaos.

And what was true for David, is true for us today. There is nothing new under the sun—the truth then remains the truth now: only by standing in the presence of God and holding our focus on One thing can we escape the chaos as the world spirals downward. Like David, we will have nothing to fear, and the attacks of the enemies will have no effect on us if we dwell in God's house, keeping our focus on Him and abiding by His principles.

But what David understood then is just as true now: if we want to seek God, we must be undivided in seeking Him. Proverbs 8:17 tells us, "I love them that love me; and those that seek me early shall find me" (KJV). Jeremiah 29:13 says, "And ye shall seek me, and find me, when ye shall search for me with all your heart" (KJV).

If we truly desire God, we need to seek Him. God promises those who seek Him with all their hearts will find Him.

Finding God

People sometimes ask me, "How come I can't find God?" The answer is because they are not earnestly looking for Him. The truth of the matter is when we really want to find something, the process we use to search for things usually results in them being found. If we lose our car keys we'll tear the house up looking for them, and most likely we'll discover many other things in the process.

God bless my wife. She had been on me a while back because I had sort of taken over a section of the house with an accumulation of all my stuff—various and sundry items of mine. There came a point that my wife couldn't take it anymore, so she decided to break it up. In so doing, she managed to find most of the stuff that I've been looking for all year! I went into the room and was amazed…

"Where was that?"

"Over there."

"Where was *this*?"

"Over there."

"Great! Thank you for finding everything."

I don't think she was actually looking for anything, but in her desire to clean, she found lots of things. She had one purpose in mind—to clean. The abundance that was found came as a result of that one purpose.

Here is my point: when we desire to find God, we're going to find a lot more. When we desire to go after the things of God, we'll be in for some surprises.

God tells us that while we're expecting to find one thing regarding Him, we will find out other things about Him as well. When we expect Him to do one thing, we will find that He does so much more than that. But it all starts when we focus on One thing—it all starts when we seek God with all our heart.

Through the Psalms, David shows us that we should have no fear in asking for God's favor and, when we are in His presence, for His blessing. Jairus understood this (Matthew 9:18–26). He knew his child was grievously ill, and he had no issue asking Jesus to come to his house to heal the child.

The woman with the issue of blood understood this (Mark 5:25–29). She had gone everywhere and tried everything and was still bleeding, so she had no problem touching the hem of Jesus' garment and, in so doing, asking to be healed. She got serious about it, and when she got serious about one thing, she did not care who was looking at her or who was talking about her.

The same was true for Jairus. He realized that his daughter was near death, but he got serious. He came for one thing, and he was set on that one thing: Jesus had to come to his house. Even after they arrived at the house and were told that the girl had died, Jairus still believed.

If you get focused on the One thing, God will show you that He is a miracle-working God. We need to first ask for His favor, though. We need to have a real desire to know Him, like David did—to dwell in His house, behold His beauty, learn His principles. One of the reasons we struggle in our desire for One thing is the fact that we just don't know. *We don't know.*

But God says to cultivate the desire to know Him, and all the other things will fall into place. God wants us to know Him and to know His Almighty Power. He also want us to fellowship with Him—to have a desire to spend time in our relationship with Him.

If I claim to be married, is it okay for me to stay away from my wife? Not to go home at all? To avoid having meals together or going places together? That wouldn't be much of a marriage, then would it?

When I was dating the beautiful woman who is now my wife, I ate more hotdogs and drank more sodas than I ever did in my life. She was selling hot dogs and sodas for the Singles Ministry. I wanted to get to know her, to talk with her, to fellowship with her. So I'd buy about seventeen hotdogs at a time, along with a case of soda. This way, I got to stand there and talk to her.

After that, I was willing to do whatever it took to stay in fellowship with her. She had me lifting cases of soda and it didn't matter how much my back hurt—I was going to do it because I wanted to spend time in her presence. I wanted that connection.

My point is, relationships require commitment and connection to work. I can't truly claim to be married if I never spend time with my wife. It's the same way with God. We can't claim our desire for God and never be in His presence. There would be no connection, no sense of fellowship.

This type of commitment requires more than just two hours on a Sunday. It requires more than a Wednesday-night Bible study or one hour of morning prayer time. God should be present in every moment of our day.

Everywhere we go, we should want the world to see our love for Jesus. Every day of our lives should be a day filled with fellowship with God. He should walk with us, talk with us, tell us that we are His and He is ours. Our desire for One thing should make it clear that we want constant contact with God all the time.

Staying on Track

We have to quit putting God on the backburner. I once heard a man say that, personally, when he gives his tithes to his church, he does it this way: the day he gets his paycheck, he writes out his tithe check first.

He doesn't want anything else to be more important than God—not his electric bill, not his car payment, not his mortgage, not even his grocery bill. Through this small act, he wants to demonstrate that, out of all the other stuff that commands his time, attention, and money, God is first.

There are so many things in this world that we think are necessities, but we can live without them. For instance, many of us think that having a car is a necessity, but we can live without a car. We might have to walk or take the bus, but we can live without that car. We love having large houses with room to put all our stuff, but we can live without lots of square feet, too.

Granted, I have a nice house now, but when I lived in New York, I saw apartments that were only a little bigger than a closet. Everything was in one room—living room, bedroom, bathroom, kitchen—all in one small space. The point is, we can live without all this external stuff we've grown so accustomed to. But the One thing we can't live without? That's God.

Fasting is one way to minimize the distractions in our lives. We've become very food-centered in our society: We have television shows about food. We see recipes posted all over the place on social media. We have so many different eating plans and programs, all designed to make us look better and feel better.

We are one of a handful of societies who have food more as a luxury than as a necessity. Many cultures, countries, and people don't focus on food because they don't have much food to think about. Yet in our culture, food has become a distraction, so fasting can be a very beneficial practice.

Fasting helps us take the focus off ourselves and satisfying our own cravings, and turns the focus back to God instead. It helps us to remember that we can do without the external stuff—even food—when we focus on the One thing that we truly can't live without. And when we become all about that One thing, that One thing will be all about us.

At some point, every believer has to answer one very important question: whether or not they are going to be saved. In the Bible, God tells us that He would rather we be hot or cold—He doesn't like lukewarm (Revelation 3:16).

One critical characteristic of God is that He will be gracious with us, but one day we will have to make a choice. We will have to choose between the external or the internal. We will have to choose between all of the stuff that surrounds us and the One thing that matters.

David himself came to that realization as he sat in his palace, holding all of the power that a king can hold. He realized he didn't want any of it. He wanted God. His true desire was for God alone. He wanted to dwell constantly in God's presence. When we come into God's presence, the other things in our lives take a back seat.

Our behavior is different in God's presence than it is elsewhere, too. For instance, there are plenty of people out there who still like to smoke. Yet if a smoker walks into my church, he doesn't light up during the service. Why? Because the rules of the house dictate no smoking.

Therefore, a smoker will refrain from smoking—a customary behavior that he does elsewhere—when in my church because the fact that he is in my presence and the presence of the congregation, prevents him from doing so. That person is restrained from his customary behavior by his environment. He can choose to leave, but his desire to be in the church service keeps him there, despite having to give up smoking during that time.

David tells us, basically, that when we become about the One thing, the environment will restrain our behavior. It will prevent us from doing things that are not good for us. There's no need to claim we can't do it—we obviously can—but it comes down to a matter of choice.

Think of some of the popular weight loss shows that are out there. People don't mind being embarrassed going on shows like that. They have no problem getting on a scale and painting themselves in a not-so-flattering light. They don't mind getting screamed at by the trainers and criticized for not losing enough weight. Why?

Because they are focused on one desire—to lose the most weight and win the prize. All of the other stuff doesn't matter, because of their primary focus.

God tells us that His ways are not burdensome (1 John 5:3). He is not out to hurt, embarrass, or humiliate us, but rather to give us hope and a future (Jeremiah 29:11). David said "As the deer pants for streams of water, so my soul pants for you, my God" (Psalm 42:1 NIV). He says that his whole being thirsts for God, longing for Him, like someone in a dry and parched land (Psalm 63:1)

This is the kind of focus we need to have. We need to fix our eyes on Jesus and see only Him. It's the only way we can break free and become all about that One thing.

WORKBOOK

Chapter 2 Questions

Question: How have you been putting God on the back-burner unintentionally, either currently or in the past? What are you putting in place of God?

_____

_____

_____

_____

_____

_____

_____

_____

_____

_____

Question: What are some things—activities, thoughts, or influences, for instance—that are truly necessary in

your life? Which things are clutter that you've been
treating as necessary?

_____

_____

_____

_____

_____

_____

_____

_____

_____

_____

_____

Question: Which items of spiritual clutter seem to be
particular obstacles in the way of your unity with God
and the Body? What is the clutter interfering with God's
purposes for you? How will you get rid of this clutter?

_____

_____

_____

_____

_____

_____

_____

_____

_____

_____

_____

Action: Stay focused on God, who is your number-one priority, and on His destiny for you. Clear the clutter out of your life—the foolishness and sin that distract you from God and your God-given purpose. Figure out what in your life is truly necessary, and what's not, as you seek out intimate time with Him and let His miracles work in your life. Today, stop putting God on the back-burner!

Chapter 2 Notes

CHAPTER THREE

Out of Many

But all these worketh that one and the selfsame Spirit, dividing to every man severally as he will. For as the body is one, and hath many members, and all the members of that one body, being many, are one body: so also is Christ. For by one Spirit are we all baptized into one body, whether we be Jews or Gentiles, whether we be bond or free; and have been all made to drink into one Spirit. For the body is not one member, but many. — ***1 Corinthians 12:11–14 (KJV)***

Have you ever examined a dollar bill? If you look closely, you'll see an emblem, which depicts an eagle clutching a fistful of arrows. The eagle is framed by the words "E Pluribus Unum." In fact, that phrase is on all of our U.S. currency, coins and bills included. It's Latin and it means "out of many, one."

It is the creed of the United States and emphasizes the fact that we are a diverse nation whose people come from many different places, many different cultures—yet we are one, united under the banner of the United States of America. What truly sets this country apart is the fact that although we are all very different, we are also one.

Different, Yet the Same

When we begin to think about the church established by Jesus, we find that, in the Bible, there are many names used to describe it. For instance, we are told that the church is:

- "The Temple of the living God" (2 Corinthians 6:16)
- "The Vineyard" (Jeremiah 12:10; Matthew 21:41)
- "Pillar and ground of the truth" (1 Timothy 3:15)
- "Sanctuary of God" (Psalm 114:2)
- "Spiritual house" (1 Peter 2:5)
- "Assembly of the saints" (Psalm 89:7)
- "Assembly of the upright" (Psalm 111:1)

And the list goes on.[2]

However, the one phrase that has probably been used most frequently to describe the church is 'the Body of Christ.' That term is a powerful description of God's intention for His church. We are, of course, all individuals, but we are so much more than that. As members of His church, we are all part of the Body of Christ Himself—living, breathing, and working as Christ Himself.

The human body is composed of many different parts—the liver, the lungs, the brain, the blood vessels,

THE POWER OF ONE · 65

the nerves, the tendons, the veins—all unique. Each part, from the largest to the most miniscule, serves an important function, and all these parts, though diverse, are designed to work together for the good of the body as a whole. And so it is with the Body of Christ—the church.

All of the parts and members of the church, large and small, are different but essential. Moreover, we are all designed to work together for the good of the Body as a whole. There is unity of purpose, and that unity is crucial to the proper functioning of any body, but especially the Body of the church.

When we look at a person, we don't see their lungs or liver or heart or blood vessels—but we know those parts are there, and we know they are functioning because we see the person as a whole, healthy individual. In the same way, when the world looks at the Body of Christ—the church—they don't necessarily see all the individual members, but what they should see is the reflection of God through us, active and alive.

One of the things God has intended is for the world to see Him through us. Many of us have been told by others, "You look just like your Momma" or "You look just like your Daddy." Our physical body displays characteristics that make us undeniably who we are. Often, others can tell who we are related to and can maybe even tell where we come from simply by watching us and by observing our physical characteristics and mannerisms.

In the same way, God wants the world to see that we are related to Him, that we, the church, are born of God. He wants the world to see that we look like our Father, speak like our Father, and behave like our Father.

Though the church is made up of many churches, God intends for us to be one in unity with Him, members of the One body, and He wants that fact to be obvious to the world around us. We may worship a little differently, but we worship One God.

So, as believers, we need to ask the question: Are we allowing God to use our diversity and our differences to serve the purpose of the church as a whole, providing a picture of unity to those around us?

Let's be clear about something—God does not want us to be uniform, but He does want us to have unity. Big difference. I tell people, one of the things that makes a cult a cult is how they insist not only in unity but also in uniformity. They make their members say the same things, wear the same things, and act the same way.

God says, "No, no, no, no! I don't want to put you on lockdown that way. Instead, I want it to be clear to the world that the freedom you have in Me is diversity, and I want you to use that diversity to help Me be manifested through the Body of the church."

Division should never be a distraction for God's church. Each and every person plays a different but vital role in the church, just as every part of the body, no matter how small, is vital. If we lose a part of our physical body, we miss that part even if we still have all the other parts. Why? Because that part plays a vital role no other part can fill. We can live without certain body parts, but we notice that they are gone and we miss them.

I used to love my hair. I thought hair was a beautiful thing. But every day that I got up and found more hair missing, I realized I could live without it. But boy, it is vital when it's cold out there! In those times, I sure do miss that hair. No other body part can keep my head warm like my hair could. It got cold last week, and I had to put a hat on. If I still had my hair, the hat wouldn't have been needed.

There are many people suffering from the cold of this world because they're missing something vital. As believers, we need to say, "God, though we may be many, if I am the vital link to someone's deliverance, if I'm the vital link to someone's destiny, God, please make sure that I'm in the Body—that they can see You through me, so that they will not perish."

Division should never be a distraction to the Body. Each member is vital to God's ministry. First Corinthians 12 is a pivotal chapter in the Bible because in this chapter, Paul is laying out how vital it is for each of us to make sure we are connected to the church and participating as a functioning member of the Body. Everyone needs to be connected to something. It seems that today there are many "extension cord Christians"—they're connected to a lot of stuff that's connected to nothing.

One of the things we have to understand is that it is not just necessary for us to come to church, but we also need to be connected to the Christ of the church. Jesus Christ should be the power—the driving force—of all that we do as the church.

I may have the privilege of serving as a pastor, but the power of the church I serve doesn't come from my personality; it comes from Christ. It shouldn't matter whether I am the pastor or not, because God's church stands on the power of Christ.

Unfortunately, what we have many times today are personality-driven people trying to build a church centered on themselves. Because of that, we have false bodies. A false body is nothing more than a mannequin. It may look nice, all dressed up, but it has no life—no spirit.

Many believers today don't have any light or power in them because they are connected to a false body—a lifeless, personality-centered church. They are not serving their function as vital members of the One true Body of Christ, and they are missing out.

I must admit that every now and then, the Lord has to deal with me to ensure I know that I'm not such a big shot. Not long ago, I was at an event with other preachers, including some very well-known preachers. Sometimes, I get used to people making a fuss over me, but no one was making a fuss over me there. No one even knew me.

It was a reminder for me that I can't allow myself to get carried away with myself, thinking I'm all that. I should instead be content to be a part of the Body and to serve the role that I serve. I can't become prideful, but rather must stay mindful that Jesus Christ is first and foremost and we are all unified in His purpose.

Christ in Action

In 1 Corinthians 12, Paul tells us that we are the Body of Christ, and the first thing that we must do as the Body is to manifest Christ in us (1 Corinthians 12:5–7).

When we look at a person, we see the outside of that person—their appearance—but we don't see the real person within, such as their personality, what they're like, or who they are. People can't see our personalities like they see our physical appearance. Instead, we rely on our bodies to manifest that personality—to show people who we are by our likes or dislikes, our actions, what we say, what we do, and so forth.

God made the church to be His Body—to manifest who He is, His personality, to the world.

In addition, Paul tells us that as the church, not only are we to manifest Christ, but we are to minister for Christ as well. Using the same example again, not only do our bodies manifest our personalities (who we are) but our bodies allow us to move and do things—to take action. That is exactly what God expects the Body of the church to do.

Not only are we to manifest His personality to the world, but we also are to take action and minister to the world as Christ would. God moves through the Body of the church.

Here's another example: Suppose there is a baby crying in the room. That baby needs something and is letting the world know by crying very loudly. Typically, someone will move, go to the baby, and give that child what she needs to stop crying and be content. But if nobody moves and everyone in that room just sits there, the poor baby will go on crying, never getting what it needs.

For us as believers, the world is crying, and we can't be content to just sit there. We, as the Body, have to move. We must give the world what it needs. We can't be content just to sit there, hoping that our manifestation of Christ's personality will be enough. Instead, we have to take action and minister to people—to those who need Christ.

In the opening words of 1 Corinthians 12, Paul says, "Now concerning spiritual gifts, brethren, I would not have you ignorant" (KJV). Why is he saying that? Simply this: He doesn't want us playing stupid when it comes to understanding the fact that we all have a role to play—we all have a spiritual gift designed to serve the Body of the church.

God doesn't want us saying, "I didn't know." He doesn't take that as an excuse. He has provided the information for us. If we don't know, it's because we don't want to know. We can't feign ignorance.

We are many, but everyone has a purpose—a spiritual gift—and we should each strive to fulfil the role we are to play in the Body. Basically, Paul is telling us, "It's clear that you should know why you're here and what you should do while you're here."

Now, let's be real about something. We may not like what we are called to do while we are here—we'll touch upon that again later—but that doesn't change the fact that everybody has a job to do. There are no unemployed saints. If we're working for Jesus, we're not holding a sign—we are *working*. And we are to work while it is day, because night is coming and when it comes, we won't be able to work.

Continuing to 1 Corinthians 12:11, we see that Paul goes on to say, "But all these worketh that one and the selfsame Spirit, dividing to every man severally as he will" (KJV). What is he telling us with this verse? Basically, he is responding to the question: If we are many, then what holds us together? How do we become one?

The answer is that we have a motivating power—the Holy Spirit. The Holy Spirit is our motivating power and the unifying force so that even though we are divided in our talents and abilities, we are One. The Holy Spirit is not divided, and He is the power that unifies us even in our diversity.

Jesus is not divided against Himself—He does not fight Himself. Of all the images and paintings we have seen of Jesus, have you ever seen one of Him fighting Himself? When Michelangelo did the mural in the Sistine Chapel, did he decide to throw an image in there of Jesus wrestling Himself?

Of course not! It stands to reason, therefore, if each of us has the Holy Spirit in us, then neither should we be divided against each other. Rather, we should be unified as One church. We are different, yes, but we are all the same in that each of us, as believers, is filled with the same Spirit. And the same Jesus who is reflected in me is reflected in you, no matter what your role is in His church.

In 1 Corinthians 12:12, Paul goes on to say, "For as the body is one, and hath many members, and all the members of that one body, being many, are one body: so also is Christ" (KJV). He's telling us here that not only do we have a motivating power, but we also have a mutual program.

What is that mutual program? It's Christ. Various churches may have different ways of doing things, and that's fine; everybody has their own style. It's fine so long as they stick with the one mutual program of serving the Body of Christ.

We can't allow our personal proclivities to cause us to miss out on the power of a mutual program. For instance, we may visit a church, and we may sit there and think "Oh, my gosh, they're going to sing that same old worship song again," or "How come they don't do a greeting like they do in that other church I've gone to?" Or something else along those lines.

But when we focus on those stylistic differences, we miss the great mysteries of God—the mutual program. The church we are visiting may sing "Amazing Grace" more slowly than we're used to, and it may take four hours to get through it, but it's still "Amazing Grace."

The point is, different churches may have different styles—they may not sing songs the way we like, they may not "do church" the way we're used to—but if they're doing it about God, then they're doing it right. They are following the mutual program.

Music won't save us, the pastor's personality won't save us, the way the church is decorated won't save us. Only Jesus can save us. That is the motivating power and the mutual program. It has to be all about Jesus and serving His Body, diverse but unified.

Today, unfortunately, it seems that we have too many "membership Christians." They like to wear the name-tag, but they're not really involved in the program.

I'm a member of a certain club right now. I pay my dues and am listed on their membership roster, but I rarely go to meetings. Sometimes they call me and ask,

"Why don't you come to any meetings? Why don't you get involved?" On those rare times when I do show up, some might even question whether I'm actually a member at all.

That's how some people are with Christianity. They wear their church membership tag and claim their name is on the list, but Christ says, "Wait a minute, are you really one of us? Why haven't you been part of the program?"

Wearing the label of Christian doesn't mean we are Christian any more than wearing a football jersey makes us part of a football team. We have to be involved in the mutual program. We must be using our gifts to serve the Body.

Every now and then, we have to give ourselves a self-assessment. We have to stop and ask ourselves, "Have I been born again, born from above? And if so, does my life reflect that fact?"

In 1 Corinthians 12:3, Paul says, "Wherefore I give you to understand, that no man speaking by the Spirit of God calleth Jesus accursed: and that no man can say that Jesus is the Lord, but by the Holy Ghost" (KJV). He's saying that at some point, our manifestation of Christ will demonstrate that we've had an actual encounter with God.

Our language betrays us. The words that come out of our mouth will serve as evidence as to whether we are true members of the Body or not. If we have had a true encounter with the motivating power of the Spirit, then our words will reflect that.

But if garbage comes out of our mouths, then what does that say about us internally? It certainly doesn't come as evidence that we are serving the one true God. Our bodies already have a place to get rid of waste, and it's not our mouths!

If we are supernaturally born again, then we are Spirit-filled, and we allow the Spirit to guide what our words and actions.

Remember Your Place

Paul tells us clearly in Romans 8:9, "Now if any man have not the Spirit of Christ, he is none of his" (KJV). If we don't have God's Spirit in us, we do not belong to Christ. It's that simple. When I hear people trying to live a life without the Holy Spirit, it pains me, because it can't be done. We can't live without blood, and the Holy Spirit is the blood of the soul. Without the Holy Spirit, we cannot hope to live.

There's nothing more aggravating than when my wife and I leave home to go someplace and I think she has something we need, while at the same time she is thinking that *I* brought the item.

"Do you have it?"

"No, I don't. Don't you have it?"

We argue back and forth, but it does us no good when we get to where we're going and neither of us has the thing we need.

The point is this: people are tired of coming to church and saying, "I thought you had it." The world is looking at the church and saying, "You guys claim to have God, but every time I come around, you don't seem to have what I need."

The Body of the church should reveal that we have everything we need to fulfill God's will in this earth. But not only should we manifest our supernatural birth, and not only should we have a Spirit-filled life, but we also should share the same love for God and, as a result, for each other.

Some people go to church out of guilt or obligation. That shouldn't be. If we are Spirit-filled, we should go to church because we love the Lord and we love His people. It's one thing to love God, but when people see that we have a genuine love for each other, they see the witness of the Holy Spirit in our lives.

How do people know if someone is losing weight? We watch them, and we see changes in them. We see the manifestation of their activity—their diet and exercise program. How about when someone gets a new hairstyle? We notice it, and the talent of the hairdresser is reflected in the beauty of the hairstyle.

Likewise, God is saying, "I intended for your body to reflect the power of the Spirit and the mutual program at work in you."

Yet if someone walked around with half of their hair styled and the other half undone, we'd notice that, too, wouldn't we? We'd notice that something wasn't right— that something was missing. Why don't people notice when the power of God is missing?

People don't tend to notice that someone is losing their hair until it is half-gone already. When I first started losing my hair, my barber said, "Mr. Pelt, your tape is moving on you." I didn't believe him.

My grandfather had a slick head on top—a skating rink right there in the middle—and bumpers on the side. I always said that would not be me. So I was in a state of shock when my barber said, "Rev, I want you to know something. You're losing something in the backyard. You might not see it through your front gate, but I can promise you, your backdoor is open."

The problem is, I never noticed it. Why? Because I couldn't see it.

How many people in this world don't realize they're losing something? They don't take heed when somebody tries to tell them that something is missing.

God has said, in effect, "I intended for the Body to manifest me." When people look at us, they shouldn't be saying, "I see your front gate, but the backdoor is open." They should see us fully covered; they should see us operating completely in the fullness of God.

And when we have a supernatural birth, a Spirit-led life, and the same love for Christ, they should see clearly that though we are many, we are One. We're not in competition. We have a shared, common life. We have a shared, common love for Christ. Christ makes it easy for us. He gives us the motivating power of His Spirit.

Keep in mind, though, as I mentioned earlier, our position in the Body is not our choice. As Paul said in 1 Corinthians 12:11, the Spirit divides "to every man severally as he will" (KJV). The Spirit decides what gifts we get and how we will serve the Body. We may have our own desires and preferences, but God is going to place us where He wants us and, at some point, our desires must yield to His placement.

Problems arise when we don't yield our desires to God's placement. Consider the story of Jonah. Jonah had a problem with placement. God wanted him to preach to the people of Nineveh, and Jonah said, "Now wait a minute, Lord, I don't want to do that." He ended up inside the belly of a fish.

The book of 2 Kings, chapter 5, tells us that the Syrian military commander Naaman had a problem with placement as well. Elisha, a prophet of God, told him, "Listen, if you want to be rid of your leprosy, go down to the River Jordan." But Naaman was thinking, "Wait a minute. I could afford some of the best spas in the world if I wanted. Why would I want to go down to the River Jordan?" He had a problem with placement, which means he had a problem with God and being part of the Body of His people.

Many of us never find ourselves being fruitful in our ministry, because we are discontent with our placement. We say to ourselves, "You mean I have to be here? But I don't want to be here."

I have worked as a substitute teacher. When I got to the school where I was substituting, I didn't tell them what class I wanted—they told *me*. Honestly, when I got to some of those classes, I didn't really want to be there. But I did the job because that's where I was placed. I had no control over the placement, but it was still my responsibility. It was where I was most needed.

If we're going to be a part of the Body, there are times we may have to get off our high horse and just accept our responsibility. God places us where He does because it is where He sees a need we can fulfill. At the end of the day, we must give an account for what we've done, including how we have handled the responsibilities and gifts that God has given us, and being unhappy about our placement will not be an excuse for doing nothing.

Unfortunately, sometimes, placement brings about pride. Many churches give titles to the positions that people hold. Personally, I don't believe in that. Titles make people crazy. For instance, in my tribe, one of the greatest debates I recall was over the term 'bishop.' 'Bishop' was a rank of ministry that afforded some opportunity. In other denominations, it denotes a person who is in charge of a diocese. So there was a great debate over whether or not we should use the title of bishop.

We did, but then some of those who held that title grew prideful. They wanted to be addressed by that title, as if somehow they were not the same person they were before they received that title. God, though, wants it to be clear that placement shouldn't give us pride. If anything, we should be proud and contented simply to be a functioning part of the Body.

Here's the reality: if there's any pride, if there's any praise, it should be for the Body as a whole, because we are all connected. God's placement of us should be for the benefit of the Body as a whole, not for our own personal elevation or edification.

THE POWER OF ONE · 79

The Power Source

While placement should not be about pride, God also wants us to understand that if we are going to be effective in our placement, we will need real power. In 1 Corinthians 12:18, we're told that God has placed every member of the Body in the way that pleases Him.

But, if that's the case, then how does each of us function effectively as a member of the Body? That question was already answered by what we were told in verse 11: "But all these worketh that one and the selfsame Spirit…" (1 Corinthians 12:11 KJV). Therefore, not only is our placement from God, but our power is from Him as well.

One of the things we need to remind ourselves is that we will never accomplish anything great for God in the flesh. I might think I'm a great preacher, and I can give wonderful oratorical speeches that may leave people impressed, but my words alone won't change their lives. It is the Spirit of the living God who brings life.

It is the Spirit who told Ezekiel to prophesy, and it was through that Spirit that the words Ezekiel spoke had the power to change lives. After the words are spoken, it is the Holy Spirit who takes those words and changes hearts. But if we don't watch our placement, we miss out on the power.

I'm an Xbox man, and when that controller is in my hand, I have the power to play the game. But if I don't put the batteries correctly in the controller, I can punch those buttons all I want and nothing is going to happen. I might have the right kind of batteries, but if they're not placed correctly in the controller, I might as well have no batteries at all.

For many of us, even when we accept the placement God has given us, we try to use His power in a way that is wrong. It's not that the power isn't there; it's just not being used correctly. God will not allow us to use His power in a way He didn't intend just for our own benefit.

The sad reality is that many people stumble and fall flat on their faces because they do not have God's power working through them in their placements. Why? It's not that God is not around, but rather that they are not ready to use His power correctly. As a result, God will not let them use His power at all.

It's just like the Parable of the Talents (Matthew 25:14–30). The parable tells us that a rich man gave certain individuals a sum of money to take care of while he went on a journey. To one guy, he gave five talents; to another guy, he gave two; and to the final guy, he gave one. The first two took the money and tried to make a profit for their boss. But the last guy was too concerned about losing the money, so he went ahead and buried the one talent in the ground, where it sat and did nothing. It stayed dormant.

When the rich man came back from his journey, he was happy with the small profit made by the first two men but was very upset with the man who just buried his money and did nothing with it. The rich man not only took the small amount of money away from the man, but he "cast ye the unprofitable servant into outer darkness" (Matthew 25:30 KJV).

This should be seen as a warning. It signifies that if we are in the Body and refuse to use our gifts, working for the good of the Body with what the Lord has given us, the Lord won't restore us. He won't revive us; He will discard us. Some of us need to ask ourselves if we are letting the power of God just lay dormant within us, because if we are, we run the risk of being cast out into the darkness as well.

I love my gallbladder—it's a part of me—but if my gallbladder acts up and starts causing all kinds of health issues with the rest of my body, guess what I'm going to do? I'm going to get that gallbladder removed so that the rest of my body can live in a healthy fashion. The Bible goes so far to tell us that if our eye offends us, we should pluck it out, and if our hand offends us, we should cut it off (Matthew 18:8–9).

When we understand how important we are to the Body, we understand also that if we don't function as intended and cause harm to the Body, then we will be removed from the Body. That's why it is so important to accept the placement God has given each of us and to let the power of God flow through us as intended.

Through God, we have placement, we have power, and we must also have participation. We can't just stand there. We have to do something.

The Body, as a whole, must participate with itself. All parts must move in a spirit of cooperation and participation. Think of it this way: When we move, our skin, our hair, our organs—they have to go with us. It's not like the skin can jump off and say, "Hey, I really don't want to go there." What a mess that would be!

The problem is that many of us are failing to understand that our placement comes with some power, and we must use that power to participate. We can't just join a church and then sit there and enjoy the show. We join a church to serve—to have a vehicle for our service to the Lord. Sure, we come to church to worship and sing and be thankful, but we are members of a church so that we have a means by which to use our placement and our power to serve God.

Even more than that, though, churches should unite together to *work* together to serve God. Just as each member of each church has a placement and a power in the church body, so does each church, regardless of denomination, have a placement and a power in the Body of Christ. It is the obligation of each church to fulfill their role within that Body, or else be cast out into darkness.

Acceptance Is Part of the Process

I mentioned previously that as a boy I suffered from asthma attacks. I'd get very sick. At those times my mother would call people to pray over me. Sometimes it would be at home, sometimes in the hospital. They weren't only people from my church—they were from all over, including different denominations. But they all worked together for a common purpose as they laid hands on me and prayed for the sickness to be gone.

They were all part of the Body, taking action according to their placement and letting the power of God flow through them to work for the greater good of the Body.

To get to that point—the point where we take action and participate as a member of the Body—we must first be able to accept ourselves. We are who we are because God made us that way, and He has placed us where He wants us, where we can do the most good for the Body. We have to be willing to accept that and stop wishing we were someone else or somewhere else.

Each one of us is beautifully and wonderfully made and created to be an imitator of Christ. The world might tell us differently. The world might tell us that we have to be different, that we have to like certain things and act certain ways—but it's a lie. Our real identity lies in Christ, and our real fulfillment lies in fact that we are meant to be unique, powerful, functioning members of His Body.

We can't force ourselves to fit into a mold that wasn't meant for us. If I go into a store and try to force myself into size 32 pants, they're going to need thirty-two people to come in and help me off the floor! We shouldn't be wearing someone else's pants—we should be wearing the pants God made for us. We are to be imitators of Jesus, but it's not one-size-fits-all.

I serve on various boards, and there are many great people on those boards. However, sometimes the people there talk so big that I feel like I need a dictionary just to follow along. Yet that doesn't mean I'm any less important on the board. In fact, I have a knack for taking whatever it is they are talking about and putting it into layman's terms so everybody else can understand what they're saying. Perhaps it's the gift of interpreting tongues!

The point is, though, I accept myself for who I am and what my gifts are, and so should every member of the Body. We are made to be different on purpose. As I mentioned before, God is not looking for uniformity—He is looking for unity.

Jesus was the perfect example of this. When He walked the earth, He knew who He was, and He knew that just because He walked with sinners didn't mean He had to be a sinner. He accepted Himself for who He was, and He accepted the sinners for who they were as well—for who God made them to be.

When I received my Master's in Public Administration, I assumed I'd be some sort of executive pastor. I was good with administration. I never thought I'd be a preacher, but God showed me that I have a gift for it. He showed me that I have a gift for getting along with people and for teaching.

I didn't expect it, but those were the gifts God showed to me. And I accepted them, and I allowed God's power to flow through me with regard to those gifts and His placement of me. I didn't shy away from using those gifts, either, because it is my obligation as a member of the Body to take the gifts God has given me and, through His power, to use them for the good of the Body.

One day, when it is my time to function at another level, then I will function at that new level. But until such a time, I'm going to be faithful where God has placed me. By being faithful over a few things, one day I may find He will give me the privilege of being master over many. I do this for one reason and one reason only:

that others may come to know the one true God. I do it for the good of the Body.

But I'm not unique in this. What is true for me is true for each one of us. We just have to be willing to accept ourselves and our placement, trust that God knew what He was doing when He assigned specific roles to each one of us, and participate in our particular role as He intended.

The process should be clear at this point. First, we have the desire for God. We seek Him above all else—seek to "enquire" into His ways and to know Him more intimately. We do that by getting connected to the power of One, so that we become one with Jesus and, through Him, one with the Father.

Then, once we are connected, we become members of the one Body, and though different, we function in unity of purpose—to serve God as He intended us to serve.

When we are connected to the Body, fulfilling the role or placement that God ordained for us, we can then let His power flow through us so we can take action in His name. Then we allow others to see Christ in us while bearing witness to the one true God.

Therein lies our identity and our fulfillment.

Chapter 3 Questions

Question: When have you experienced discontent with your place in God's plan? How did you (or how can you) come to embrace your place in the Body?

_____

_____

_____

_____

_____

_____

_____

_____

_____

_____

_____

Question: In what specific ways could you start participating more actively and meaningfully in the Body of Christ—in His church?

_____

_____

_____

_____

_____

_____

_____

_____

_____

_____

_____

_____

Question: Where besides Christ do you sometimes try to find your identity? What particular steps do you need to take to shed these false sources of identity and re-embrace your identity in Christ?

_____

_____

_____

_____

_____

_____

_____

_____

_____

_____

_____

Action: Accept yourself so you can embrace your place as a member of the Body of Christ. Instead of being yet another Christian in name only, participate actively in His Body. Work together with other members of His church to be Christ in the world. In all of this, look to Him alone as your source of power and identity, not to any earthly position—not even within the church.

Chapter 3 Notes

_____
_____
_____
_____
_____
_____
_____
_____
_____
_____
_____
_____
_____
_____
_____
_____
_____
_____
_____
_____
_____
_____
_____
_____

THE POWER OF ONE · 91

CHAPTER FOUR

Needing One Another

*A new commandment I give unto you, that ye love one another; as I have loved you, that ye also love one another. By this shall all men know that ye are my disciples, if ye have love one to another. — **John 13:34–35 (KJV)***

No building is made of one single brick. Rather, buildings are constructed of many bricks, built one upon the other, supporting each other to form a structure that is strong and firm. That's how God intended His church to be built as well.

While we are all meant to experience the power of One, we are not meant to do so alone. We need one another. God intended His church to be a place where the world could see fellowship in action. Through His church, the world can see people of diversity, people of different cultures, of different colors, of different backgrounds, and so forth, all come together, unified under the banner of Christ.

No Lone Rangers

There's no such thing as a stand-alone believer. God saves each of us, and out of many, He makes One. The One is made up of many members, each supporting the other. Different roles, same purpose, but also interdependent.

Every now and then, Christians fall prey to isolation; they believe they can go it alone. They want to be in church, but they don't want to be around church people. They don't want to be held accountable for their behavior outside of church. They may even view "church" as a part-time thing, but when they want to go out and have a good time, they put their church relationships in their back pocket for a while and go about doing their thing.

This is not what God intended. Church is not a part-time thing. Our relationships with other believers are meant to be the cornerstone of our lives. The church Body is not made up of a bunch of perfect people, but rather of a group of imperfect believers who are perfected through their salvation in Jesus Christ. Once truly connected to the Body, life apart from the Body ceases to be a reality. And each member of the Body is designed to support the others.

I've mentioned this before, and I'll mention it again: God doesn't want uniformity; He wants unity, and it is through this unity that all stand firm. We all need others to help us get through life and to reach our full potential. None of us can do it alone. We weren't designed to do it alone.

Even Kool-Aid needs water to become what it was meant to be. With God on our side, with the power of God flowing through us, even though we don't look alike, even though we don't live in the same place, even though we don't like the same things, there's nothing that's going to stop me from loving you and helping you be all that God wants you to be.

We need other people. We were meant to connect with other people. That's how we are designed. Consider Adam in the Book of Genesis. He had the whole garden, with all the animals, and even got to commune with God Himself. But guess what? He discovered that despite everything that he had, he still needed another human being to feel whole, connected, and complete.

In the Bible, the phrase "one another" is used over seventy times—fifty times in the New Testament alone. Do you think God is trying to tell us something? We need one another. Why? For a few reasons.

First, we need one another for *safety*. The Bible tells us when two or three are gathered, great things can happen. A single thread can be snapped easily, but when you wrap three threads together into a cord, it is not as easily broken. Jesus never sent any of His disciples out alone. They always went together, at least with one another and usually with others.

When the Apostles went off on their own, things usually didn't go so well. Think about Judas—he went off on his own when he betrayed Jesus. It ended with him taking his own life. What about Peter? He was on his own when he was sitting in the courtyard the night Jesus was arrested. What happened then? He ended up denying Jesus three times.

For our own safety, and for our own good, we should not go it alone. Even the Lone Ranger, despite his name, had Tonto, didn't he?

Second, we need one another for *sufficiency*. It is God's will that every need of His house be supplied out of His house. If you don't help one another, as members of the same Body, we all suffer.

I have a younger brother. I may be older, but my brother was always bigger and more gifted in many ways. When we were boys, my father would routinely give us jobs to do. I'd always get right to it, and I'd be working hard, trying to keep from getting a whupping.

So this one time I was doing my best, working as hard as I could, but I was never the best at following instructions. Despite how hard as I was working, I was doing it all wrong. My brother was good with instructions, and he knew the right way but said nothing. Along came my daddy, who took one look at me and asked, "Man, what in the world are you doing?"

"I'm doing what you told me to," I said.

"Didn't your brother tell you how I said to do it?"

"No, sir. He did not."

Then my brother piped up and said, "Well, you were working by yourself, I just figured I'd let you do it your way."

And I got hot and asked him, "You mean you knew all the time what I needed to do and that I was doing it wrong, but you wouldn't help me?"

"Well," he said, "you never asked."

From what I've seen, some people in the church take on the same attitude my brother had that day. They see a brother or sister struggling with their assignment from God, but they offer no help even though that brother or sister is going about it all wrong.

We don't have to wait for our brothers and sisters to ask for help. Instead, we should be there for one another, ready to help—to provide for their safety and sufficiency because, as members of the One Body, when one member suffers, we all suffer.

While we are all designed for service, we serve better when we serve together, working together toward a common goal. Consider your hand. It is one hand comprising five digits. Separate, yet connected. The pinky has some strength and can lift some things, but it can't lift nearly as much as the hand as a whole, with all the fingers working together.

Like the fingers of the hand, while we each have our own strengths, we are designed to work together, to help and serve one another in order to glorify God in a world in which so many do not even believe that God exists. The church is not a place of competition; it's a place of completion.

God gave each of us our own spiritual gifts. But how can we learn to use our gifts if we stay in isolation? How do we learn to use the gift of encouragement unless we go to people and encourage them? How do we use the gift of teaching unless we surround ourselves with people to teach? How can we use the gift of prayer unless we come together with people to pray for them?

Love Like God

The phrase "one another" is a critical phrase for believers. If we're truly believers, we need to love everybody. Love is a choice, not a feeling, and as believers we choose to love one another, to look after one another, and to support one another as members of the Body. That's exactly what Jesus is telling us in John 13:34–35. He is giving us a new commandment, which is to love one another.

God speaks of love all throughout the Bible, beginning with Genesis. But this time, it's a little different. What we're told is that He wants us to love one another as He loves us. That's a different standard than many of us use. Many of us love others on our own terms. We put conditions on it. We find reasons not to love someone and ways to limit the love we show. But that's not God's standard.

God so loved the world that He gave up His only Son to be tortured and murdered so that we, the unworthy sinners, could be saved—so we could be made whole again, heirs to His Kingdom. God does not put conditions on His love. God's love forgives, even in the face of injustice. God's love gives, even when we don't give back. It is real love, whole and pure and unconditional.

This is how He loves us. And this is how He wants us to love one another. It's a new standard—and it's not a suggestion; it's a commandment.

We are commanded by God to love one another as He loves us. If we are not loving each other, we are not obeying God's commandment. This kind of love has nothing to do with liking somebody. We are commanded to love even those we don't like. Why? Because Jesus died for everybody—not just the people we like, but the ones we don't like as well.

Everyone shares in the opportunity for salvation, and Jesus invites everyone to become members of the Body. And when they are members of the Body, we become connected to them. The Holy Spirit fills them, and it is our obligation as believers to love them. It's got nothing to do with liking them or not. The Jesus in me loves the Jesus in you!

Loving one another is a commandment. And it is also a confirmation. Love will make us shut our mouths even when we have the change to say something bad about someone else. Why? Because love builds up, it does not break down.

Love covers a multitude of faults, my faults and yours. It lifts us up, and it lifts those around us up as well. When the world sees us loving like that—loving unconditionally and unquestioningly—the world will see Jesus through us.

In Romans 15:7 Paul tells us, "Wherefore receive ye one another, as Christ also received us to the glory of God" (KJV). What does this mean? That love does not run people off. Instead, it draws people in. So when Jesus starts drawing people in through love, guess what we should do? Receive them!

For those who have experienced childbirth, we know the process is not pretty. It's messy, and it's painful. But that doesn't stop the doctor from receiving the baby from the mother. And no matter how messy that newborn is, the mother wants to hold and love on that baby. All they see is the beauty of new life.

New birth in Jesus Christ can be messy and painful, too, but that should not stop us from receiving the one who is being reborn. God doesn't ask us to clean up the mess, but He does ask us to receive the person and to love them despite the mess, just as He loves us regardless of *our* messiness. God confirms that when we commit to loving others, when we allow His Spirit to love through us, then we don't see the mess either—all we see is someone getting delivered, being saved.

If we speak badly about people, just remember that they can turn around and speak badly about us, too. There are no perfect people here on this earth, myself included. We all come with our own messes and God accepts us where we are, mess and all.

The Lord has been very gracious and kind to me, but I haven't been saved all my life. There are some things in my background that might raise an eyebrow or two, but God received me all the same. His love is unconditional. Our love of one another should be unconditional, too, not based on what we consider "too messy" for our tastes.

Giving Up Some Personal Space

We have to love one another. We have to receive one another. We can't be afraid to get close to one another as members of the Body. Take a look at what Paul says in 1 Corinthians 16:20: "All the brethren greet you. Greet ye one another with an holy kiss" (KJV). Paul is not advocating a kissing contest here. Basically, what he is telling us is that if we receive one another and love one another in Christ, then we must allow each other into what we consider our personal space. Why? Because our personal space isn't personal anymore.

In some cultures, one of the customs when you enter someone's house is to greet the head of the house with a kiss. I went to an Indian church and a Romanian church, where it was mandatory upon entering to greet the head of the church with a kiss—not just touching cheeks, but a kiss with the lips.

In our culture, many of us are kind of nervous about that stuff—it seems a little too intimate for us. But in those other cultures, and especially in the churches, if a person is not willing to share a holy kiss, they are not ready to receive another as a member of the Body. The kiss is an outward demonstration that we are ready to relinquish that personal space and get close to other members of the Body.

God tells us that a holy kiss is a transmission of blessing, for out of the abundance of the heart, your mouth speaks. So our mouth should be a blessing to others because it speaks from a heart filled with the Spirit. A holy kiss is an expression of this.

We have to be willing to get close to one another so we can receive one another and pronounce a blessing through a kiss. It's a demonstration of love and confirmation that others are safe with you—you will not harm them or gossip about them, but will uphold them and encourage them.

I used to love the old-time preachers. Not only were they smooth, but they always had good breath. The one I remember in particular always had Dentyne. Not only were his words a blessing, but I didn't mind getting close because his breath was clean and pleasant. When we are filled with the Spirit, or words should be clean and pleasing to others—a blessing that invites the intimacy of a holy kiss.

In 1 Corinthian 12:25, Paul also tells us that "there should be no schism in the body; but that the members should have the same care one for another" (KJV). So, if we are ready to greet each other with a holy kiss, then we should also be ready to care for each other as well. God tells us that even though there are parts of the Body that may have more prominence, they all get the same protection.

Consider this example: Some parts of our bodies get more attention than others. I know some ladies love to get their nails done. They love to have the manicures and the pedicures and show off their beautiful nails. I know some men who pay special attention to their hair, making sure they style it just right and that it hides all of the spots that might have become a little sparse.

But even though these parts of the body might receive more attention, when we come to protecting the body, we protect all parts equally. If we go out into the cold, we make sure we're all covered up. If we run away from danger, our whole body runs, not just our hair or our nails. We protect all of the parts of our body, not just the prominent ones.

That's what God is telling us—there should be no schism. All of us are members of the One Body and serve the same God. We need to care for each other equally, regardless of prominence or position.

We need to be willing to do whatever it takes to care for one another as members of the same Body. When my foot hurts, I give it the same amount of care as I would if my hand were hurting. If one part of my body hurts, the rest of me doesn't feel well, either. Even something as small as a splinter in my pinky finger can disrupt the rest of me. It's all I can think about, the pain in my finger caused by that splinter, and nothing seems right until I take care of that injury.

These are the clear signs that the Spirit of God is truly working within us: we love one another, we receive one another, we greet one another with a holy kiss, and then we ask God to give us the strength to care one for another.

Many of us don't care for one another because care costs. It costs time, it costs money, and it requires commitment. Caring for one another might mean we have to open our homes and make accommodations for someone else. It might mean that we have to cut back on some of the things we like to do to so we can pay for something that someone else needs.

Sometimes we are the ones who need to be cared for, in which case we must be willing to accept that role as well. We need to be willing to allow others to care for us as members of the Body so that *they* can be blessed. But then, when the time comes for us to care for another, we can't ignore that responsibility, either.

It's a two-way street, and we have to be ready to meet the needs of others when and where we can. Caring is not often convenient, because meeting the needs of others usually requires sacrifice. But when we truly choose to love each other, we must also choose to care—because caring for one another is love in action.

Submission and Salvation

Ephesians 5:18–21 tells us:

> *And be not drunk with wine, wherein is excess; but be filled with the Spirit; speaking to yourselves in psalms and hymns and spiritual songs, singing and making melody in your heart to the Lord; giving thanks always for all things unto God and the Father in the name of our Lord Jesus Christ; submitting yourselves one to another in the fear of God.* **(KJV)**

God wants us to speak to one another in psalms and hymns from the heart—in other words, He want us always to speak to each other in an uplifting, encouraging way, from the Spirit, that fills our hearts. Then, He tells us that He wants us to submit to one another. Let's consider for a moment what that word 'submit' really means.

The Greek word for 'submit' as used in Ephesians is *hypotassō*, which literally means "to arrange under" or to get in order, subject to another, as a solider might be arranged within the structure of an army.[3] More specifically, in this context, it means to subject oneself to the order God has arranged. In other words, we should not make determinations as to who is first, who is last, who is better, or who is worse. Rather, we should order ourselves according to God's design.

If God sees fit to bring His Word through the mouth of a child, I can't be so big-headed as to say, "Now hold on there, brother, I'm the pastor and God's words should come through me." The moment I get to this point, I'm out of line. I'm not in order—I'm not submitting.

Sometimes we may be first in line, sometimes we may be last, and sometimes we may be somewhere in the middle. The point is, though, it doesn't matter where we are in the line. We are all members of the Body, and we need to submit to one another—not insisting that we be ahead of everyone else, but rather desiring to serve and care for one another because all are of equal importance.

The bottom line: we should treat everyone as important, submitting ourselves to them by loving and caring for them.

Submitting ourselves to each other means confessing to each other as well. Here are the rules of confession:

If we do something publicly that is wrong, we confess it publicly to those who are affected by our wrongdoing.

If we commit a personal wrongdoing, we confess it to the person we have offended.

If we have done something wrong privately (we committed a sin that doesn't involve other people, but hurts our relationship with God), then we confess it to God.

We all make mistakes. Keeping our mistakes to ourselves does not foster forgiveness, and if we share a holy-kiss level of intimacy with members of the Body, we should not be afraid to admit when we have been wrong. If the wrong we have committed is in public, then we need to confess our sin in a public setting.

I can recall a time when a particular television preacher did something wrong and betrayed the public trust. The apology was done publicly, televised for those who were wronged to see. Similarly, if a pastor has done something wrong that has hurt his congregation, he needs to confess the wrongdoing to his congregation. It's not enough just to confess to the church leadership—he needs to confess to those he has wronged.

In the same way, if we have wronged someone personally, then that needs to be confessed and addressed with the particular person we have hurt. For instance, if I step on my Brother Jimmy's foot, I don't go to Jimmy's wife to apologize, nor do I tell her to tell Jimmy I'm sorry. I don't go on Facebook or send Jimmy a text to tell him I'm sorry. No—I go to Jimmy face to face and confess that I did wrong and that I am sorry.

Such face-to-face confession is part of the connection and that intimacy that God wants us to have as members of the Body. Confession requires submission and is a necessary expression of our love and connection with each other.

Finally, if we sin privately in a way that does not hurt another person but hurts our relationship with God, we need to confess that sin out loud to God and ask Him to change our heart. We also need to ask Him to help us search our heart—to help us see whether that sin we consider private did, in fact, hurt someone else in some way. Sometimes, the sins we think are private affect others around us without us realizing at first.

Regardless of the specific circumstances, confession is not an easy thing. It requires submission, and it requires trust. As believers, if someone wrongs us and confesses to us privately, we have to keep it private. There is a part of us that wants to tell everyone all the dirty details. We must resist that impulse, however, because otherwise we undermine the trust that comes with love and submission.

Therefore, we need to guard our tongue and resist the urge to tell everybody everything. Our words can ruin people, and our words can ruin us. That's why we must keep the Spirit in us and speak *through* the Spirit, so that He can be the One who guards our words when we cannot.

As believers, not only do we have the obligation to confess, but we also have the obligation to forgive. We are told to forgive others as God has forgiven us (Matthew 6:14–15). That's some pretty deep forgiveness. And if someone confesses a wrongdoing to us, it is not for us to reserve our forgiveness and hold the whole thing over their heads. In fact, Jesus warns against doing so in Matthew 6:15, telling us that if we withhold forgiveness, God will withhold His forgiveness from us.

That's a pretty sobering thought, isn't it? If God withholds His forgiveness of our sins, then where is our salvation? So along with confession, as members of the Body, we are also to forgive one another.

Church is not a place for perfect people. We all need forgiveness because we all make mistakes. Church is a place for imperfect people who are going on to find perfection in Christ. That's why it all starts with love. Love is the only thing that will allow us to carry on no matter how badly we've messed up.

I'm a father, and my wife will tell you that even though our children are grown, they are still our babies. If they need something, we are going to be there for them. Likewise, God is saying that every soul out there, every single person, is His child. No matter what His children do, no matter how badly they mess up, He will have a place for them if they call for His help.

And God wants His church to be a reflection of that love—a community in which, no matter where a person comes from or what a person has done, we will be there to receive them, greet them with a holy kiss, love them, care for them, and forgive them.

How can we do all of this? Through the power of One. It all starts there. When we seek God earnestly—when we seek to know His Will and His ways—we will find the connection that Jesus Himself prayed for us to find. We will become unified as One, and God's own Spirit will flow through us, filling us with His power so we can become effective members of the Body.

When that connection becomes a reality for us, we will find the love that allows us to care for, submit to, and forgive one another. Then, the rest of the world can see the Body of Christ in action, as it was meant to be.

WORKBOOK

Chapter 4 Questions

Question: What are some specific ways in which you need God? In what specific ways do you need other members of the Body?

_____

_____

_____

_____

_____

_____

_____

_____

_____

_____

_____

Question: What is one way you could better love others by reaching outside of your comfort zone?

_____

_____

_____

_____

_____

_____

_____

_____

_____

_____

_____

Question: How often do you confess your sins to God? To whom in the Body do you need to confess particular sins today?

_____

_____

_____

_____

_____

_____

_____

_____

_____

_____

_____

Action: Remind yourself daily that you can't do life alone. You need God and His Body, and you need to love others as God does. Start caring more about what God wants and what others need than you do about your personal space and staying in your comfort zone. For instance, practice confessing your sins to God and to others in the Body. In all things submit to the Lord—and let Him save you.

Chapter 4 Notes

CONCLUSION

The Power Beyond the Surface

Every now and then, we are with a person in a certain setting and we don't know who that person really is.

When my family and I first came back to Florida, our ministry was just being formed. My wife was heading to a First Ladies Conference in West Palm Beach. So, while she was away, I got invited to a meeting of pastors in a town called Manalapan. I had never heard of that town, but since my wife was away, I figured I might as well go.

We stayed at a nice hotel there, I remember, and as the week went on, we were invited to the house of one of the preachers, someone whom I had already met. Since I didn't know the area at all, I drove with some other pastors who knew their way around.

As we were driving, I was thinking to myself, "Where in the world are we going?" The houses were getting larger by the mile. We turned onto a road, and there in front of us was a huge gate, something you'd expect to see out in Hollywood. I was riding in my old green Suburban, and as I saw all these nice cars rolling up, I was starting to get nervous, feeling a little out of place.

We entered the house, and the kitchen was as big as the church I pastor. Everybody was in the kitchen, about fifty people just standing around, and it didn't even feel crowded! Then we were told to make our way to another room, and I was thinking to myself, "There's another room?"

We all wandered into the next room, which was as big as my church times two. I like kids, and there was a little boy in the room, who asked if I'd come play with him. Of course, I couldn't refuse. So he took me to another part of the house, and as we were walking along, I was wondering if we were even in the same building anymore.

The boy turned to me and said, "Don't worry, if they need you, they'll call you over the intercom." Which was fine, except at that point, I didn't know if I'd be able to find my way back!

Well, as it turns out, they did page me over the intercom, and I did eventually find my way back. When I did, I looked at the pastor who owned this home in a whole new light.

I had thought I knew him, but I really didn't. I had a very limited view of who he was based upon my limited interactions with him. After our meeting, I saw him differently, not just as a humble pastor, but as the owner of a wonderful mansion—one which he was willing to share with us all if we were willing to follow him there.

Recall John 17:24: Jesus says, "Father, that they may also see the glory that I had from the beginning." Think about what Jesus is really asking here. Basically, He's saying, "Father, I have been with these disciples, but they still really don't know who I am."

Jesus looks at His disciples and realizes that they really don't know Him—at least not as He truly is. So He asks the Father to "glorify Me together with Yourself, with the glory which I had with You before the world was" (John 17:5 NKJV).

When we understand the glory God has, He'll be glad to change our story. He'll be glad to open our eyes to a world we would never have imagined.

The Bible tells us that God is "the author and finisher of our faith" (Hebrews 12:2). We may not know where we are going, but when we open ourselves up to the power of One, God will rewrite our story and steer us to a place where we will be filled with His glory—so that we can reflect it back to others.

I want the power of One. I want to be connected with the Father as Jesus is. I want to be connected with heaven like Jesus is. I want to be connected with the things above like Jesus is. Why? Because it is the only way that my story on this earth is going to make any sense.

God's glory causes faith to grow—our faith and the faith of others. God's glory causes grace to be realized. Glory makes us understand that if it weren't for His grace, we would be lost. That's why grace is so amazing—it is the key to salvation. God's glory gives grace freely.

It changes us. Isaiah said, "I am a man of unclean lips, and I dwell in the midst of a people of unclean lips" (Isaiah 6:5 KJV). But the moment he connected to God's glory, he was changed. Not because of his own doing, but because of God.

A short time ago, the Holy Spirit spoke to me as I was washing dishes. I was washing a pot that I had burned pretty badly. I had put a potato in the pot to cook it, but fell asleep. When I woke up, the potato had burned up the bottom of the pot. I ate that potato, anyway—that's how hungry I was—but then I had to deal with the burnt pot.

And as I was scrubbing away, the Holy Spirit spoke to me and said, "Son, this is how the life of a believer is. Nobody washes dishes with just water. You put soap and water in. But do you realize, after you wash the first dish, that water is dirty?

"Even though you have soap in it, there's the residue of what was there before. Yet you are still trying to clean your dishes with water that is dirty."

The reality is, Jesus is the only person who can deal with the residual grime that's left inside of us. He is the only one who can get us clean from sin.

The fact remains that if we don't tap into the power of One—if we don't align ourselves in unity with God—we'll be tossed to and fro by every wind or wave or doctrine that comes along.

If we don't tap into the power of One, we will never be able to serve as an effective witness for Christ.

If we don't tap into the power of One, we will not succeed in our endeavors, because nothing can be done apart from God.

When we yield to the power of One, however, we allow ourselves to be aligned with God, as Jesus intended, and to shine with His glory for all to see. Our lives will be redeemed by grace and redefined—reshaped in accordance with God's purpose. What could possibly be better than that?

REFERENCES

Notes

1. Isidore, Chris. "Target: Hacking Hit Up to 110 Million Customers." *CNN Money*. 11 January 2014. http://money.cnn.com/2014/01/10/news/companies/target-hacking/
2. Torrey, R. A. "Titles and Names of the Church." *The New Topical Text Book*, 1897. In *Bible Study Tools*. http://www.biblestudytools.com/concordances/torreys-topical-textbook/titles-and-names-of-the-church.html
3. "Strong's G9253 – hypotassō." In *Blue Letter Bible*. https://www.blueletterbible.org/lang/lexicon/lexicon.cfm?t=kjv&strongs=g5293

About the Author

Bishop Anthony Pelt is a native Floridian who earned his B.A. in Political Science and his Master's in Public Administration at the University of Central Florida. An ordained bishop, he is the Founding Senior Pastor of Radiant Living Worship Center.

Bishop Pelt has served on several local, state, and international boards, including Youth and Christian Education, Seminary Board of Theology, and the General Assembly Cabinet for the Church of God.

Bishop Pelt is a man who truly loves the Lord, serves the Lord with gladness, and is committed to implementing solid biblical teaching in ministry—to elevate the people in everyday living outside of the church walls with strong belief that "Christian Education is the key to Church Elevation for the total man."

Bishop Pelt has preached throughout the States, Canada, and the Caribbean Islands.

Bishop Pelt has implemented several annual evangelism outreach events, including Community Day, at which free health screenings, Blood Bank Mobile, Mammogram Mobile, a clothing drive, prayer, and food are provided. This event normally serves over 200 people.

Christmas in Grenada, another of these evangelism outreach opportunities, involves purchasing items like shoes and clothing for over 250 children. These items are shipped to Grenada to provide Christmas for needy children. Bishop Pelt also supports the Angel Tree project for kids in the community whose parents are incarcerated.

He has also implemented Man-Up Monday, in which men from all around the community come together to share and encourage one another in dealing with any issues they may face.

Bishop Pelt is a community activist and serves as a voice of reason for many people and groups throughout the community. Because of his passion for education and evangelism, he has now adopted the county schools in our city to provide school supplies, book bags, tissues, and hand sanitizers for students who are less fortunate. He also provides a petty cash fund for the local elementary schools to ensure that no child goes without eating at school.

He currently serves as Chairman of the Deerfield Beach Housing Authority. He is a volunteer chaplain for the Broward County Sheriff's Office, a volunteer for Broward

County Public Schools, and a guest speaker and mentor for the Jim Moran Youth Automotive Training Center in Deerfield Beach, Florida. He is the past president of the Deerfield Beach Christian Ministerial Association.

Bishop Pelt was recently appointed by the Church of God International Headquarters as the Administrative Bishop for Florida-Cocoa.

He is married to Millicent and has three children—Imani, Tyrone, and Hope.

About Sermon To Book

SermonToBook.com began with a simple belief: that sermons should be touching lives, *not* collecting dust. That's why we turn sermons into high-quality books that are accessible to people all over the globe.

Turning your sermon series into a book exposes more people to God's Word, better equips you for counseling, accelerates future sermon prep, adds credibility to your ministry, and even helps make ends meet during tight times.

John 21:25 tells us that the world itself couldn't contain the books that would be written about the work of Jesus Christ. Our mission is to try anyway. Because in heaven, there will no longer be a need for sermons or books. Our time is now.

If God so leads you, we'd love to work with you on your sermon or sermon series.

Visit www.sermontobook.com to learn more.

www.ingramcontent.com/pod-product-compliance
Lightning Source LLC
Chambersburg PA
CBHW061831040426
42447CB00012B/2917